C000155070

Social Conte ⌐... ⌐uency in L2 Learners

NEW PERSPECTIVES ON LANGUAGE AND EDUCATION

Series Editor: Professor Viv Edwards, *University of Reading, Reading, Great Britain*
Series Advisor: Professor Allan Luke, *Nanyang Technological University, Singapore*

Two decades of research and development in language and literacy education have yielded a broad, multidisciplinary focus. Yet education systems face constant economic and technological change, with attendant issues of identity and power, community and culture. This series will feature critical and interpretive, disciplinary and multidisciplinary perspectives on teaching and learning, language and literacy in new times.

Recent Books in the Series

Distance Education and Languages: Evolution and Change
Börje Holmberg, Monica Shelley and Cynthia White (eds)
Ebonics: The Urban Education Debate (2nd edn)
J.D. Ramirez, T.G .Wiley, G. de Klerk, E. Lee and W.E. Wright (eds)
Decolonisation, Globalisation: Language-in-Education Policy and Practice
Angel M. Y. Lin and Peter W. Martin (eds)
Travel Notes from the New Literacy Studies: Instances of Practice
Kate Pahl and Jennifer Rowsell (eds)

Other Books of Interest

Bilingual Education: An Introductory Reader
Ofelia García and Colin Baker (eds)
Continua of Biliteracy: An Ecological Framework for Educational Policy, Research, and Practice in Multilingual Settings
Nancy H. Hornberger (ed.)
Developing Minority Language Resources
Guadalupe Valdés, Joshua A. Fishman, Rebecca Chávez and William Pérez
Language and Identity in a Dual Immersion School
Kim Potowski
Language and Literacy Teaching for Indigenous Education: A Bilingual Approach
Norbert Francis and Jon Reyhner
Language Learning and Teacher Education: A Sociocultural Approach
Margaret R. Hawkins (ed.)
Language, Space and Power: A Critical Look at Bilingual Education
Samina Hadi-Tabassum
Language Minority Students in the Mainstream Classroom (2nd edn)
Angela L. Carrasquillo and Vivian Rodríguez
Multilingual Classroom Ecologies
Angela Creese and Peter Martin (eds)
Disinventing and Reconstituting Languages
Sinfree Makoni and Alastair Pennycook (eds)
Understanding Deaf Culture: In Search of Deafhood
Paddy Ladd

For more details of these or any other of our publications, please contact:
Multilingual Matters, Frankfurt Lodge, Clevedon Hall,
Victoria Road, Clevedon, BS21 7HH, England
http://www.multilingual-matters.com

NEW PERSPECTIVES ON LANGUAGE AND EDUCATIC
Series Editor: Viv Edwards

Social Context and Fluency in L2 Learners
The Case of Wales

Lynda Pritchard Newcombe

MULTILINGUAL MATTERS LTD
Clevedon • Buffalo • Toronto

Library of Congress Cataloging in Publication Data
Newcombe, Lynda Pritchard.
Social Context and Fluency in L2 Learners: The Case of Wales/Lynda Pritchard
Newcombe.
New Perspectives on Language and Education
Includes bibliographical references and index.
1. Language and languages–Study and teaching–Social aspects–Wales.
2. Welsh language–Study and teaching–Social aspects. I. Title.
P53.8.N43 2007
306.4409429–dc22   2007006871

British Library Cataloguing in Publication Data
A catalogue entry for this book is available from the British Library.

ISBN-13: 978-1-85359-995-8 (hbk)
ISBN-13: 978-1-85359-994-1 (pbk)

Multilingual Matters Ltd
UK: Frankfurt Lodge, Clevedon Hall, Victoria Road, Clevedon BS21 7HH.
USA: UTP, 2250 Military Road, Tonawanda, NY 14150, USA.
Canada: UTP, 5201 Dufferin Street, North York, Ontario M3H 5T8, Canada.

The policy of Multilingual Matters/Channel View Publications is to use papers that
are natural, renewable and recyclable products, made from wood grown in
sustainable forests. In the manufacturing process of our books, and to further support
our policy, preference is given to printers that have FSC and PEFC Chain of Custody
certification. The FSC and/or PEFC logos will appear on those books where full
certification has been granted to the printer concerned.

Typeset by Techset Composition Ltd.
Printed and bound in Great Britain by the Cromwell Press Ltd.

To Robert

"All the second language speakers known to me achieved fluency by abandoning or even ignoring the formal learning process and voluntarily immersing themselves in the company of native speakers. Motivation is a hard thing to measure, but these people definitely have it, for they are subject to all the pressures to which so many others succumb. It is not of course simply a question of endurance. Successful learners are those who manage to find a successful set of strategies for coping with the stress."

Carol Trosset (1984: 48)

"I went to three or four lessons but I learned in the community after that. I would not speak so well without the help of the community. Just going to class is not enough."[1]

Alice Traille James (2002)
Welsh Learner of the Year 2002

"I don't think there is anything sadder than seeing someone who has learned Welsh and is fairly fluent leaving a learning institution without knowing how they are going to use[2] *Welsh from then on because it is not in a class that one learns a language but through using it."*

Helen Prosser (2005)
Senior Lecturer in Welsh at the University of Glamorgan,
Former Director of Teaching at the Welsh Language Teaching Centre, Cardiff University

1. This and all subsequent quotations translated from the Welsh are italicised throughout the text. Welsh quotations are to be found in Newcombe and Newcombe (2001b) and Newcombe (2002a, 2002c).
2. The words 'practise' and 'use' are used interchangeably throughout the text reflecting the observation of one of the participants that, when students speak Welsh in the community, it is often difficult to distinguish between what is use and what is practice.

Contents

Acknowledgements

I owe a great debt of gratitude to the students who agreed to participate in the longitudinal study of Welsh learners. They gave willingly of their time to take part in a pioneering research venture in Wales. Without them this book would not have been possible. Language learners from Cardiff and elsewhere who did not participate in this project have also enhanced the research by providing language autobiographies and perceptive comments on the research.

Many tutors, tutor organisers, other professionals, language learners, and friends have given of their time to read all or part of this book and have offered valuable insights. They are too numerous to list here, but I am very grateful to them all. I am particularly grateful to my husband, Professor Robert G. Newcombe for his statistical input, constructive observations, and consistent support. Finally, I would like to thank Professor Viv Edwards who has been more than conscientious as an editor and without whose encouragement this book may well not have been written.

Glossary

Abbreviations

ALTE	Association of Language Testers in Europe
AWLP	Adult Welsh Learners' Project
CILT	The Centre for Information on Language Teaching and Research
ELWa	Education and Learning Wales (In 2006 taken over by the Welsh Assembly Government)
EFL	English as a Foreign language
ESL	English as a Second Language
HMI	Her Majesty's Inspectors
LEARN	Centre for Lifelong Learning, Cardiff University
MYM	*Mudiad Ysgolion Meithrin* [Nursery Schools' Movement]
NAfW	National Assembly for Wales
NIACE	National Institute of Adult Continuing Education
S4C	*Sianel Pedwar Cymru* [Channel Four Wales]
SLA	Second Language Acquisition
TEFL	Teaching English as a Foreign Language
TESOL	Teachers of English to Speakers of Other Languages
WAG	Welsh Assembly Government
WCC	Welsh Consumer Council
WEA	Workers Education Association
WfA	Welsh for Adults
WLB	Welsh Language Board (In 2006 taken over by the Welsh Assembly Government)
WJEC	Welsh Joint Education Committee
WTC	Willingness to communicate

Welsh Terms

CYD	A society that aims to bring Welsh-speakers and learners together to socialize. Literal meaning: 'together'.
Cynghanedd	Welsh poetry in strict metre
Eisteddfod	Festival of the arts

Gorsedd	A bardic order which admits those who have made a substantial contribution to Welsh language and culture. Literally means throne.
Mudiad Ysgolion Meithrin	Nursery Schools' Movement
Sianel Pedwar Cymru	Channel Four Wales
Ti a Fi	Mother and Toddler groups. Literal meaning: 'You and I'
Ysgol feithrin	Welsh-medium nursery school
Merched y Wawr	A society for women similar to the Women's Institute in other parts of the UK. Literal meaning: 'Women of the Dawn'.

Foreword

For many years, I have been in frequent touch with teachers and researchers living under the shadow of the belief that to overcome the dramatic effects the Franco dictatorship (1939–1975) had deliberately inflicted on the Catalan language, all that was needed was its return to its rightful place as the language of the schools. Once all young people learned it, hey presto! the language's wounds would be miraculously healed.

The truth is that, as the numbers of people, especially the young, who attained literacy in Catalan reached historically high levels, surveys have repeatedly shown that the spontaneous, social use of the language has failed to follow suit, even in Catalonia itself. Adult learners complained bitterly about the lack of support they obtain among their Catalan-speaking interlocutors, many, if not most, of whom continue to conform to the predominant social norm of speech accommodation[1] (Street & Giles, 1982; Woolard, 1989; Shephard *et al.*, 2001) by actually switching from one language to another.

And yet, despite the negative message such practice conveys to potential learners, adults in Catalonia, many, if not most, of them native speakers of other languages, have continued to flock to Catalan classes by the thousand.

When I first heard Dr Pritchard Newcombe explaining some of her Welsh research, I immediately realised that she was unknowingly hitting the nail on the head regarding many phenomena familiar in the Catalan context. By getting qualitative feedback from her respondents' diaries and journals in the Adult Welsh Learners' Project, her first-hand insights are of relevance well beyond the Welsh geographical and linguistic context.

Moreover, her comprehensive overview of the outcome of relevant research in Wales and elsewhere is of great value both inside and outside the country. At the time of writing, a Chair in Multilingualism set up at the Universitat Oberta de Catalunya and sponsored by the Casa de les Llengües -Linguamón[2] has started to operate. One of its first aims is to share the results of research on what leads to successful language learning, and particularly, what has a bearing on a key factor, the 'willingness to communicate'. It is comforting, though not surprising, to find Dr Pritchard Newcombe referring in her book to the work of Richard Clément, Robert Gardner and Peter McIntyre, among others.

For languages like Catalan or Welsh, a successful educational system, though being far from all that is required, is certainly a necessary condition for their health in the global age. The importance of adult learners, however, should not be underrated. Their motivation is clearer, the obstacles they face are vivid, and when they describe their experience, their insights can be extremely useful to those responsible for language policy making and implementing. This is, to my mind, the greatest contribution of this book. Rather than magical solutions, what it offers is real down-to-earth experience.

Let me save my last words for the adult learners themselves. This book should greatly bolster your efforts. Many others (and not just in Wales) have been through the same moments of elation and disappointment before you. They have faced, and overcome, the same kinds of challenges as you. I am sure this book will help you keep your spirits up, and help others in the same community to give you more active support. The book can play the same kind of role the longstanding *Bilingual Family Newsletter* plays for its many readers.

Thank you, adult learners, and thank you again. If, and when, concerns about the future of our languages (Catalan, Welsh, and so on) increase, you will be there to tell us, firmly, to be confident in the future. You are investing in the language, you feel it is worthwhile. Let not others, then, falter! *Diolch yn fawr iawn!*

Miquel Strubell

Notes

1. Speech Accommodation Theory has been re-termed Communication Accommodation Theory.
2. A body set up by the Government of Catalonia with the aim of promoting the world's languages as a vehicle for communication, civilisation and dialogue, a source of personal development, human creativity and heritage of mankind, and to promote the rights of individuals and of linguistic communities. See www.linguamon.cat

Chapter 1
Introduction

The focus for this book is adults learning Welsh in Wales, a country where the majority of the population speaks English – not Welsh – as their first language. A central theme is the experience of learners outside the safety of the classroom. In the tradition of writers such as Norton (1998), R.O. Jones (1999), Norton and Toohey (2001), MacIntyre *et al.* (2001) and Tarone (2004), great emphasis is placed on the learner as a social being whose processing of the second language (L2) depends to a large extent on their ability to negotiate entry into the social networks of target language speakers.

The issues I will be discussing in relation to Wales, however, have clear implications for a wide range of other situations where the population is bilingual or multilingual and where communication takes place in a language of wider communication, for example, in English in the Netherlands or Scandinavia, and in French in Francophone Africa. Although most speakers from outside the language community in question choose to use a language of wider communication in settings of this kind, those who make the effort to learn the local language often feel frustrated and discouraged when local people reply in the language of wider communication. This frustration is intensified in locations such as Wales, Friesland, and the Basque country, where those who speak the minority language have equal or nearly equal proficiency in the language of wider communication.

The basic thesis of this book is that successful language learners require regular interaction in the target language in a setting in which they feel comfortable. For many people, however, this aim is extremely difficult to achieve. In many situations, native speakers of the target language are reluctant to provide the necessary practice for learners. Language learners in the United States, for instance, despite the availability of English speakers, sometimes report acquiring conversational English from television programmes and advertisements rather than real life interlocutors (Liu, 1984). It requires time and patience on the part of the native speaker to hold a conversation with a second language learner, because of the latter's accent and time taken to recall.

English-speakers wishing to learn another language face additional challenges. Such is the appeal of learning English that many interlocutors will persist in using English rather than their mother tongue, despite the best efforts of the English-speaking learner. This has certainly been my personal experience. A fairly fluent German speaker, I kept a diary on visits to Germany and noted that most Germans who were able switched to English. A great deal of determination was required to persuade interlocutors to converse in German (Newcombe, 2001). Ann Allen (2004) reported similar experiences when learning Arabic in the Sudan as colleagues were eager to improve their English skills. Yet naturalistic practice is vital if L2 learners are to become fluent L2 speakers. Loveday's (1982) studies of Spanish and Italian immigrants to Germany noted that the most important factor in their mastering the German language was contact with Germans, more important even than the length of time they had been in Germany or their age on arrival.

Learners of Lesser-Used Languages

Welsh is one of a very large number of 'lesser-used languages' and the fact that it is used by a relatively small number of speakers creates special challenges for language learners. Recent decades have, however, witnessed an increased interest in the preservation of lesser-used languages. As N. Jones (1992: 126) comments: 'All over Europe there is a surge of adults learning minority languages seeking "small is beautiful"'. Even Luxemburgian, spoken by fewer than 300,000 as a first language, is now held in higher regard and the production of literature for adults has grown considerably since the early 1980s, despite the high prestige in which French and German are held in Luxembourg (Fehlen, 1999). Moreover, intensive programmes are set up to teach lesser-used languages such as Basque and Catalan (Beardsmore, 1993: 49). There has also been interest in the renewed promotion of dialects, for example *Plattdeutsch* [Low German] in Northern Germany (Unidentified, *Institut für Niederdeutsche Sprache*, 1982).

Even North America, known for its widely held 'English Only' *Weltanschauung*, has witnessed a renewed interest in preserving and promoting some of the threatened languages of the First Peoples. For instance, at the University of California, Macri (2004) has set up a programme to promote Native American languages and, in Canada, the First Peoples' Cultural Foundation (2003) has established an on-line programme to help preserve and revitalise the languages of aboriginal peoples. In New Zealand, there is an increase in the use of the Maori language amongst young people (Benton &

Benton, 2001) brought about mainly by the emergence of Maori-medium (immersion) schools inaugurated and managed by the Maori since the 1980s (May, 2000). O. Davies (1992: 76) is probably right in anticipating that as a result of 'a battle being fought all over the world we are entering a new age in which what is local, small and human will receive the respect it is due'.

The support of native speakers is particularly crucial in the learning of lesser-used languages. In the case of Wales, for instance, there are large areas, such as the capital Cardiff and its environs – the main location of this study – where the only contact for many learners with Welsh is in a class-room and the rest of life – home, social and work – is conducted through the medium of English. In situations of this kind, learners have to seek opportunities to meet Welsh-speakers and converse. Disappointing encounters in the early days discourage some people from using the lan-guage in a naturalistic setting; consequently they only ever speak 'class-room Welsh', resort to simply reading the language, or give up altogether.

In addition, learners of a lesser-used language often battle against the feelings of inferiority that afflict native speakers who may have a heightened awareness of the low status of their mother tongue. Such feelings may result in comments such as, 'They can't seriously want to be fluent in our language', or in the notion that all learners speak a majority language therefore there is little point in speaking to them in their newly acquired lesser-used language.

Those committed to preserving language diversity need to understand that adult learners have a vital role to play. With writers such as Crystal (2000), Romaine and Nettle (2000) and Dalby (2002) warning of the almost certain demise of thousands of lesser-used languages during the 21st century, adult learners – and in particular those who wish to transmit the language to their children and grandchildren – clearly need to be nurtured (B. Jones, 1993).

Why Wales?

Of the six Celtic languages, Welsh is the most used in the community (O'Neill, 2005). The survival of Welsh and its increased use in a variety of new domains has been an inspiration to many speakers of lesser-used languages world wide. The Welsh language has become a leading example of the reversal of language decline (Abley, 2003) and Welsh has had a higher profile in the media in the UK in recent years (Rogers, 2006). The new millennium has witnessed an interest in Wales' success with bilingual education and language revitalisation. Visitors from many different regions and countries have been impressed by Wales' political and linguistic schemes. For example, a Corsican television company has filmed in a variety of locations, a TEFL lecturer in Japan has commended Wales' progress towards bilingualism (Childs, 2004) and a delegation of Iraqi Kurds, a group whose language has been greatly oppressed, has come on a fact finding mission to Wales (Unidentified, 2004: 32).

In order to understand the success of language planners and activists in Wales, we need to look first at the factors affecting the fall and rise of the language.

A brief history of Welsh

The Acts of Union of 1536 and 1542 had made Wales officially a part of England and subsequent legislation excluded Welsh from the public domain. This resulted in the Anglicisation of the upper classes who needed to use English if they were to be socially acceptable in England and upwardly mobile. Thus, the Welsh language became linked with the lower social classes. However, the language was remarkably robust for centuries, largely due to the translation of the Bible into Welsh in 1588 and the social and cultural life that centred around Welsh language chapel life.

At the beginning of the 19th century, Welsh was spoken by the majority in Wales and monolingualism was the norm. It was only as the century progressed that the language came increasingly under threat from English. There were a number of reasons for this. An important one was the impact of a British Government Commissioners' report of inquiry into the state of education in Wales (known generally as the 'Treachery of the Blue Books') (1847), which attributed most educational, social, economic and cultural disadvantages to the maintenance of the Welsh language.

The payment of teachers by results for English and Maths (but not Welsh) and the introduction of free compulsory education through the medium of English in the 1870s also played a part in the ongoing decline of the language. In addition, English was increasingly associated with personal advancement and Welsh was discouraged in educational establishments. Other factors militating against Welsh language use were high rates of immigration into Wales consequent to the burgeoning industrial economy; the loss of lives in World War I; the increased influence of the English language as people became more mobile; the migration of Welsh-speakers from Wales due to economic factors, in particular the depression in the 1920s; migration from rural 'Welsh heartland areas' to Anglicised urban areas within Wales and beyond in search of employment; the growth in the English language media; and the secularisation of Welsh society leading to a decline in chapel attendance and, thereby, the loss of a variety of chapel-based Welsh-medium social events and networks (Aitchison & Carter, 2000; Janet Davies, 1999; Jenkins, 2000a; Jenkins & Williams, 2000; John Davies, 1993; R.O. Jones, 1999; Williams, 1990). In 1901, 49.9% of the population spoke Welsh, many of whom were monoglot. By the 1991 census, however, only 18.7% claimed to speak Welsh fluently.

Equally, a large number of developments have played a part in the reversal of language shift, for which an important catalyst was a radio broadcast in 1962 by one of Wales' key littérateurs and language activists, Saunders Lewis, warning that if Welsh were to survive into the 21st century drastic action should be taken for its preservation, particularly in official domains. Although many were working to promote the language at this time, this speech was the trigger for widely-publicised non-violent protests and campaigns (Price, 1985).

Arguably, the most important influence in the fight to restore the Welsh language in the latter half of the 20th century has been education: the very institution that contributed so powerfully to its decline. In the face of considerable skepticism and hostility, educationalists and parents campaigned relentlessly for the right for children to be educated through the medium of Welsh (Williams, 2003). Over 450 primary schools and over 50 secondary schools now offer at least part of the curriculum in Welsh. The language also plays an important role in English-medium schools where it became a compulsory subject for all students from age 5 to 14 in 1988 and is now compulsory to the age of 16. There is also a flourishing bilingual school outside Wales in London (Clark, 2005). Welsh-medium schools have gained an enviable reputation with parents for high educational standards. Johnstone (2006) has argued that some of the innovative developments in Wales, such as immersion for children and adults, may offer insights for many other contexts.

Despite the great measure of success enjoyed by Welsh-medium education, there are reasons for caution. Evidence from several sources suggests that language ability does not always translate into use and that pupils tend to use Welsh less as they grow older (Baker, 1992). Intergenerational transmission is a vital element in the promotion of endangered languages with writers such as Fishman (1991) and Edwards and Newcombe (2005a) arguing against relying exclusively on the school as the main agent of language maintenance and shift. Similarly, Gruffudd (2000) draws attention to the importance of creating opportunities for young people to socialise and be involved in leisure activities through the medium of Welsh. *Urdd Gobaith Cymru* [The Welsh League of Youth], for instance, has embarked on a three-year action plan to persuade children to use Welsh with their peers (Davies, 2005a).

Great strides have also been made since the 1960s in the Welsh presence in the media. The same influences that initially worked to the detriment of the language by introducing English into homes where otherwise only

Welsh would have been heard, namely radio and television, have ultimately become a force promoting the language, but only after considerable pressure. In 1937, a BBC radio Welsh Home Service was established. Initially, it broadcast mainly in English, with only around five hours per week in Welsh; by the mid-1960s there was an output of around 25 hours per week. In 1977 the combined radio service was split into channels broadcasting in the English and Welsh languages; by 1984, Radio Wales was broadcasting approximately 72 hours per week in English and BBC *Radio Cymru* [The Welsh medium radio channel] around 80 hours per week in Welsh (Hume & Pryce, 1986: 332–333).

Although by the 1960s television had become widespread in Wales, BBC Wales only produced six hours of Welsh programmes per week and the independent channel for Wales and the West of England only five and a half hours. In 1982, following much pressure which culminated in a hunger strike by Gwynfor Evans, the first *Plaid Cymru* [Welsh Nationalist] MP, there emerged a new channel, *Sianel Pedwar Cymru (S4C)* [Channel 4 Wales], which included all the Welsh language programmes. *S4C* currently broadcasts in Welsh for over 30 hours per week, mainly at peak viewing time, and is also available digitally.

Menter a Busnes [Enterprise and business] was set up in 1989 and seeks to develop the role of business in contemporary Welsh language and culture. It delivers a range of programmes aimed at inspiring young people and Welsh-speakers to think creatively about business opportunities and to start new businesses. *Ffatri Fenter* [The Enterprise Factory] offers young people practical ways of running an experimental company in a supportive, controlled risk environment.

Several decades of language activism led to the establishment in 1988 of the Welsh Language Board (WLB), an advisory body for the language. Subsequent to the 1993 Welsh Language Act, which requires that public bodies make provision for the equal use of Welsh and English, WLB has been authorised to not only promote the use of Welsh but to also ensure its adoption in the public sector. The devolution of power in 2000 from the United Kingdom government in Westminster to a Welsh Assembly which sets the political agenda for WLB has also helped foster more favourable attitudes towards the language: the official target for the number of Welsh-speakers by 2011 is an increase of five per cent (Welsh Assembly Government, 2002).

In order to achieve this target, WLB language planners have initiated a number of highly innovative projects. The *Mentrau Iaith* [language initiatives], for instance, were established in 1991 in communities containing a high proportion of Welsh-speakers. A *Menter* is a local organisation that offers support to communities to increase and develop their use of the Welsh language. Each *Menter Iaith* offers a range of services depending on local needs (Williams, 2001). There are now over 20 such ventures throughout Wales in areas with high and low proportions of Welsh-speakers. The Cardiff venture, which began in 2000, seeks to stimulate Welsh in a wide social context as well as amongst Welsh learners. Its language strategy aims to ensure increasing Welsh for Adults (WfA) provision in the city and that more employers introduce vocational training through the medium of Welsh (Kiff, 2001).

Iaith Gwaith [Work Language] was a direct response to research conducted by the WLB which demonstrated that Welsh-speakers and learners want to know who can speak Welsh so they can use the language in their daily lives. The use of the *Iaith Gwaith* logo on badges, counters and in shop windows shows customers that Welsh services are available. Badges for learners who lack confidence ('*I'm learning Welsh*') are also available.

Twf [Growth] is a project that encourages parents to transmit the language to their children, and works with Welsh learners and speakers. While various language minority communities are addressing language transmission in the family in a piecemeal way, the *Twf* project represents the first serious attempt to tackle this issue on a strategic level. *Twf*'s message – that bilingualism is something that parents should aspire to for their children and that the ability to speak another language increases children's life opportunities – may reverberate not only with parents in Wales but in a wide range of other settings. Interest has already been expressed in adapting the *Twf* publicity materials for use in South Africa, with Hispanic communities in the United States, with an indigenous North American language, and with minority languages in Canada (Elaine Davies, 2005; Edwards & Newcombe, 2003, 2005a,b).

WLB is giving growing priority to the marketing of the language. 'Work, play, live . . . Use Welsh' – the latest marketing message – stresses the usefulness of the Welsh language in all aspects of life. The campaign targets English speakers and Welsh learners using a variety of media, including a series of TV advertisements, billboards on buses across Wales, and a dedicated website: http://www.workplaylive.org/ (Williams, 2004).

The current situation

By the beginning of the 21st century, the relentless pattern of language decline had not only been halted but had started to reverse. The 2001 census showed that 20.8% claimed to speak Welsh fluently (see Figures 1.1 and 1.2). There are many Welsh-speakers in other parts of the United Kingdom, especially in London, and in other countries, in particular the United States

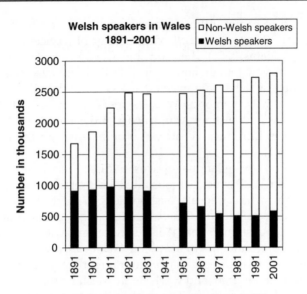

Figure 1.1 Welsh-speakers in Wales 1891–2001 (*Source*: Data extracted from Janet Davies (1993: 53–68) and 2001 census data)

and the Welsh colony of Patagonia in Argentina, although no definitive statistics on the numbers of speakers are available (E. Jones, 2000; Jones & Jones, 2001; R.O. Jones, 2001).

Scholars, however, envisage the future of the language in widely different ways. Some, such as Jenkins (2000b), view the demise of Welsh as inevitable despite the vast strides of recent decades. The latter half of the 20th century has witnessed the fragmentation of the traditional Welsh heartlands in North and West Wales and, according to Jenkins, neither educationalists nor politicians can save a language which, in an increasingly mobile society, is constantly bombarded by English both in the community and in the media. C.H. Williams (1994: 139), on the other hand, believes that the fears regarding the demise of the language have been greatly exaggerated and that the fact that England's closest neighbour and first colony should re-establish its identity through a language struggle is: 'a latter day miracle in a world suffused with concepts of globalisation, economies of scale, profit and world systems'. Moreover, if Welsh becomes established in new domains, such as the business, legal, and private sectors, Williams argues that, the 21st century may well witness a fully bilingual Wales, where the option to speak, write and read in Welsh is secure. (For a fuller discussion see Newcombe, 2002c.)

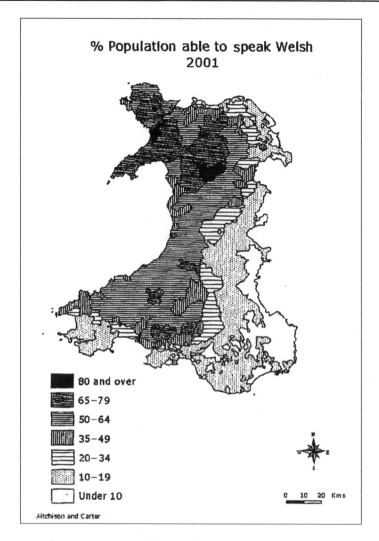

Figure 1.2 Percentage population able to speak Welsh, 2001 (*Source*: Aitchison and Carter, 2004: 52; map reproduced by permission of Y Lolfa)

European policy on the cultivation of linguistic diversity, as well as the growing global interest in preserving endangered languages, provides additional succour. However, the battle remains to be won, both in the rural heartlands which are losing Welsh-speakers and in the cities and towns in the Anglicised South East of Wales where they are migrating. Urban areas do not generally inspire the same emotional and community bonds associated with rural areas. Welsh certainly has a much higher profile than it did in the mid 20th century but its long term future remains uncertain.

The capital: Cardiff (or *Caerdydd*)

Cardiff, the capital of Wales, is the main location for the empirical data reported in this study. At a time when the heartland areas are disintegrating rapidly and contain a fragmented core of Welsh-speakers, it is encouraging that the number of Welsh-speakers in the capital rose from 9623 in 1951 to 32,504 in 2001, an increase only partially due to boundary changes and population growth. Welsh-speakers now comprise 11% of the population of Cardiff. This is a substantial change since Morgan (1955) described Cardiff as representing 'an alien sophistication' for many Welshmen, where 'Welsh is seldom heard apart from on the lips of the highly educated in-migrants'.

In 1955, when the city was formally designated as the capital of Wales, there were calls to give Welsh a higher profile in government and in administration. The creation of the Welsh Office in 1966 and, from 1982, the increased use of Welsh in the media, generated job opportunities for Welsh-speakers in the city. These factors, together with the presence of the National Museum and the Museum of Welsh Life and further opportunities for Welsh-speakers in the law courts of the city as a result of the Welsh Language Acts of 1967 and 1993, resulted in migration from the Welsh heartland to the capital by upwardly mobile professional people. These migrants tended to settle in the traditionally middle to high status residential districts of the city and support Welsh-medium education.

The increased use of Welsh in the capital needs, however, to be seen in perspective, since English still has a dominant influence on daily life. Nonetheless, the increasing emphasis on the use of Welsh in official domains is likely to lead to a more overtly Welsh Cardiff over time. And, if the attachment to Welsh-medium education continues in the next generation, the bilingual nature of the capital is likely to become even more evident. Cardiff's hope lies in establishing Welsh in relatively new or revived domains, by building on the gains of Welsh-medium schooling and the contribution of adult Welsh learners.

The Present Study

The analysis of the challenges facing adult language learners in the following chapters draws on data from a wide range of studies for which I was responsible over a period of four years, in what I will refer to as the

Adult Welsh Learners' Project (AWLP). Unlike many other studies on language learners, students were recruited from classes run by Local Authorities and voluntary groups as well as colleges and universities, thus ensuring a wide perspective on adult Welsh learners.

An important source of data is learner journals.[1] Arguments for using diaries and journals as research instruments are well documented (see, for instance, Bailey, 1991; Bailey & Nunan, 1996; Benson & Nunan, 2004; Cohen, 1998; Nunan, 1989; Peyton & Reed, 1990): they generate data that may be inaccessible through other research techniques and can help establish what is 'significant to learners'.

I also draw on a range of other data sources for the AWLP study: questionnaires completed by participants in Cardiff, National *Eisteddfodau*[2] and at an intensive residential course in Lampeter; participant observation in classes where I was the teacher and in Welsh-medium nurseries where adult learners were present; semi-structured interviews with learners, tutors and tutor organisers; focus groups discussions; and card sorting exercises where students were asked to rank the difficulties they faced in learning Welsh and follow-up questionnaires on interviewees (see Table 1.1). In addition, I interviewed four WfA professionals with considerable experience of teaching Welsh to adults, as an additional source of information for triangulating with the experience of the students.

As can be seen in Table 1.1, some of the participants in Cardiff took part in multiple activities: these formed the core of the AWLP.

Table 1.1 Number of learners by setting and nature of study

Instruments	Eisteddfod 1998	Eisteddfod 1999	Lampeter 1999 Intensive Residential	Cardiff 1998–2000
Questionnaires	55	14	19	175
Diaries				29
Interviews	3			16
Journals				10
Dialogue journals				4[3]
Focus groups				10
Card sort				14
Observation at nursery				3
Follow-up postal questionnaire				14

Several issues are salient for an understanding of the positions taken by participants in relation to the learning of Welsh and, therefore, their inclusion in Table 1.2. The levels in the second column refer to the proficiency of students at the time they participated in a questionnaire study at the beginning of their involvement in the AWLP. It should be noted, however, that students sometimes attend classes inappropriate for their level. For example, someone who has been learning intermittently for many years may attend an intermediate class although they have the knowledge to attend an advanced. For present purposes, students are categorised as Advanced (A), Intermediate (I), Beginner (B) and Intensive (Int), namely, someone who has attended an intensive course (see Chapter 2). The sample does, however, also include *Siop Siarad* (SS) students whose main aim is to build confidence in speaking: some have attended beginner courses, or an intensive course and others have been learning intermittently for many years.

Age is potentially a salient factor for two reasons, firstly because of controversy about the optimum age for language learning (see Chapter 7) and secondly because attitudes towards the Welsh language in society as a whole have changed considerably over the last four decades. The ages of the key participants in the AWLP are spread relatively evenly across younger, middle-aged and older adults.

Having Welsh in the family is a particularly salient factor. It is defined for present purposes as having heard Welsh fairly regularly from a family member in their youth, rather than being of Welsh ancestry. This experience ensures that adult learners will already have a small reservoir of vocabulary on which to draw as well as models of pronunciation.

Students who have or have had children in Welsh-medium schools have ideal practice opportunities and may have a strong integrative motive (see Chapter 7) to continue learning. Students who intend to enrol their children in Welsh-medium schools may have similar motivation.

A final salient feature to be considered is the language used by learners when interviewed, in journal writing and in follow-up questionnaires. Language choice is not always determined by the length of time of learning or level of proficiency but rather by the learners' confidence in using the language (see Chapter 5). Their choice of language is therefore an excellent indicator of their level of confidence.

Structure of the Book

Chapter 2 describes the phenomenal growth in adults learning Welsh in the latter half of the 20th century. A discussion of the characteristics of adult

Table 1.2 Student profiles[4]

Name	Level	Age	Welsh in family background	Partner Welsh-speaker	Children in Welsh school	Language use at interview	Language use in journal	Language use on follow-up questionnaire
Agnes	I	Elderly	No	No	No	Mixture	Welsh	Welsh
Alan	A	Middle-aged	No	No	Yes	Welsh	Mixture	English
Alice	B	Young	No	No	No	English	Mixture	English
Cathy	A	Middle-aged	No	Yes	Yes	Mixture	Mixture	English
Clare	B	Middle-aged	Yes	No	No	Mixture	Mixture	English
Kim	A	Middle-aged	No	Yes	Yes	Mixture	Mixture	Welsh
Laura	B/Int	Young	No	No	No (intends)	English	English	English
Ray	B	Middle-aged	No	Yes	Yes	English	Not relevant	Not relevant
Rees	I	Middle-aged	Yes	No but learning	Yes	Mixture	Welsh	Welsh
Roger	I	Middle-aged	No	No but learning	Yes	Mixture	English	English
Sally	A	Young	No	No	No	Welsh	Not relevant	Not relevant
Sioned	I	Young	Yes	No	No	English	English	English
Andrea	SS	Young	No	No	Yes	English	English	English
Lydia	SS	Young	No	No	No	English	English	English
Philip	SS	Elderly	No	Yes	Yes	English	Mixture	English
Sharon	SS	Young	No	No	Yes	English	English	English

learners provides the backdrop for a description of the range of provision and accompanying methodologies which have emerged over the years. Emphasis is placed, however, on the importance of consolidating the learning that takes place in class through use in the community.

Chapter 3 concentrates on problems students encounter in the community. Drawing on autobiographical and biographical accounts of learners and data from the Adult Welsh Learners' Project (AWLP), it highlights four main challenges for learners: the tendency of native speakers to switch to English, the speed of speech, dialect differences, and code switching and mixing. It also explores anxieties of native speakers and the impact of these anxieties on L2 speakers.

Chapter 4 discusses issues of culture and identity and their bearing on language learners' decision to continue learning the L2.

Chapter 5 considers ways in which learners' lack of confidence and anxiety affect their willingness to use the L2 outside the classroom. It examines the extent to which anxiety is a trait associated with the learning situation or the individual learner.

Chapter 6 moves from attitudinal barriers to practising Welsh in the community to the more practical issues of time and opportunity which act as barriers to using the language. It examines two inter-related aspects of time: student expectations of how long it is likely to take to learn a language; and how much time is available for study. Questions of opportunity are also discussed, particularly in relation to lesser-used languages such as Welsh.

In Chapter 7, the focus is on motivation for – rather than obstacles to – successful language learning and why motivation is not always sustained. In particular, the discussion focuses on two key questions: Who are the adult learners of Welsh? And what are their motives for learning the language?

In Chapter 8, I conclude that the relevance of social context in the development of L2 fluency is a vital area for research and recommend that more work on learner preparation, learner strategies and native speaker preparation be undertaken in Wales and elsewhere. Further study of the practice patterns of successful learners is also recommended since a clear understanding of what enables some learners to build on the skills gained in lessons outside the classroom may help those who fail to progress from L2 learner to speaker.

Notes

1. Instructions to journal writers following Pierce (1993) are included in Appendix A. The instructions were presented to participants in both Welsh and English.
2. The National *Eisteddfod* (plural *eisteddfodau*), a competitive festival of the arts of considerable cultural and linguistic importance, is held annually for eight days, alternating each year between diverse venues in North and South Wales.

3. *Siop Siarad* students. A *Siop Siarad* is a class that usually meets once a week and consists of learners with a command of the fundamental grammar constructions and a fairly wide vocabulary who wish to meet to practise Welsh. No summative assessment takes place.
4. Pseudonymic Christian names are used to protect anonymity of students in the AWLP. All other learners' contributions use learners' actual names.

Chapter 2
Adult Language Learners

Introduction

This chapter looks at adults in general: the characteristics they share and the challenges they face for teaching and learning, particularly in relation to languages. It traces the phenomenal growth of Welsh for Adults (WfA) since the 1970s, both through intensive language classes modelled on the Israeli ULPAN and through other forms of adult provision. Important links are made between consumer demand and the language methodologies and materials that emerged during this period. Finally, attention is focused on issues adult learners confront when they make the transition from the classroom to the community in an attempt to consolidate their language skills.

Characteristics of Adult Learners

The orthodoxy amongst continuing educators has been that adult learning and learning early in life have identifiably different characteristics. Knowles (1978), who remains an important influence in current debates, argues that adults have a vast reservoir of knowledge on which to draw and that the teacher should not be an instructor but a facilitator, assisting students to learn in a self-directed way. This image of the practical, focused and self-directed learner holds true for many adults. Certainly, all adult learners need appropriate content, materials, and activities that meet their needs and interests and allow them to demonstrate their skills and abilities. However, Rogers (2002), drawing on 40 years' experience in the field, is more doubtful that adult learning and learning early in life have identifiably different characteristics and trajectories. He attaches more importance to the distinctions between task-conscious and learner-conscious learning, and between informal or non-formal learning and formalised learning. Rogers (2003) calls for more research to clarify these issues.

In spite of philosophical differences of this kind, most scholars would agree that adult learners have a number of characteristics in common:

- Adults are usually able to assume responsibility for themselves. They are used to taking decisions and setting goals in their daily lives. Consequently, they may resent being directed by the tutor and accommodating to the needs of the group.
- Adults bring a stockpile of knowledge and experience to the learning situation – life experience gained over years. Some of this experience will facilitate their current learning.
- Adults also bring thought patterns, attitudes and set ways of coping with things to the learning situation. Although these behaviours are generally advantageous, dogmatic attitudes and a lack of flexibility may hinder the development of some adults.
- Adults may lack confidence in themselves as learners and under-estimate their own powers. They may be over-anxious and reluctant risk-takers. Such attributes will vary according to the personality of the learner and previous learning experiences. It may take some time for learners who have negative memories of earlier learning to build confidence.
- Adults, particularly those with little formal education, do not normally realise how long learning a new skill can take. They often expect too much too quickly and put themselves under unnecessary pressure.
- Adults normally learn on a part-time basis. They have many responsibilities outside the classroom and may not be able to allocate much time to their studies outside class, however motivated they are.

The characteristics outlined above can apply to all kinds of adult learning; some, however, may have particular importance for language learning. Anxiety is a particular hindrance, since speaking, especially in the early stages of language learning, will not usually be fluent or accurate. The anxious learner will fear appearing foolish in front of the group and may be unwilling to take risks (Beebe, 1983). However, it is widely believed that learners need to take risks and accept mistakes as a constructive part of the learning process if they are to progress to fluency (Arnold, 1999).

Welsh for Adults (WfA)

The adult Welsh learner was a neglected species in the first half of the 20th century and few studied the language formally. Those who did tended to be intellectuals, such as the writers J.R.R. Tolkien and Gerald Manley

Hopkins and the politician and classicist Enoch Powell, who used the language acquired for written rather than oral communication (Newcombe, 2002c). It was widely held that to become a fluent speaker one had to learn the language in childhood or not at all (Kinney, 1992; Martin-Short, 1998).

The 1960s saw a radical transition in the approach to teaching Welsh to adults, as changes in classroom strategy encouraging oral/aural rather than written work enabled learners to communicate more effectively with native speakers. In the following few decades, the numbers of adults enrolled on Welsh courses provided by universities and Local Authorities grew at an astonishing rate (see Figure 2.1), from 5000 in the academic year 1972/73 to over 20,000 each year from 1996/97, with record enrolments of more than 25,400 in 2004/5. R.O. Jones (1993: 577) has predicted that, if the rate of growth in learners continues, there could well be more second-language Welsh-speakers than native speakers in the foreseeable future. Over the same period, there has been an increase in the number of Welsh learners outside Wales, particularly in London, Patagonia, and the United States, some of whom spend time in Wales in order to practise their Welsh language skills (E. Jones, 2000; Jones & Jones, 2001; The Centre for Information on Language Teaching and Research (CILT), 2005). Exact figures for 1994/5 onwards are presented in Table 2.1 but only rounded figures are available for the earlier years in Figure 2.1. The statistics reported here include students enrolled in

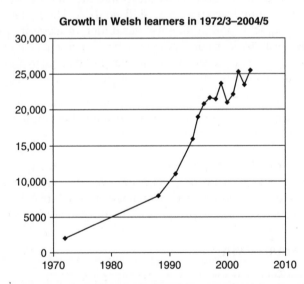

Figure 2.1 Growth in Welsh learners 1972/73–2004/05 (*Source*: 1972/3: Rees (2000: 27), 1988/9 and 1991/2: Prosser (1997: 95), 1994/95–2004/05 (ELWa))

Table 2.1 Enrolments on WfA courses 1994/5–2004/5

Year	Total
1994/5	15,894
1995/6	18,966
1996/7	20,762
1997/8	21,643
1998/9	21,500
1999/00	23,634
2000/1	21,011
2002/3	25,324
2003/4	23,483
2004/5	25,465

both intensive and non-intensive courses provided by universities and Local Authorities but do not include voluntary and private sectors. Because they may include students who have enrolled more than once, the actual number of students could be fewer. However, many other students, not accounted for here, are participating in distance learning and web-based courses and learning informally with friends and family.

A revival of interest in the Welsh language in the Welsh colony of Patagonia, Argentina, has followed the same pattern. In the 1970s, in a radio broadcast in Patagonia, Professor R.O. Jones reported that he was witnessing the death of the language; the same observer more recently expressed amazement at the new-found pride in the area's Welsh heritage with even Argentinians of non-Welsh descent, such as Sandra de Pol, Welsh Learner of the Year 2001, learning the language (R.O. Jones, 2002). However, he is aware that similar problems face learners outside class in Patagonia as in Wales. Persuading native speakers to give learners the much needed practice is also problematic in Patagonia (R.O. Jones, 2006).

Welsh classes started in 1991 with intensive courses run by native-speaking tutors. Sponsorship of tutors from Wales by the Welsh Office, now the National Assembly for Wales (NAfW), began in 1997. In 2000, there were over 700 learners, including 234 adults, though numbers later decreased because of the acute political and economic problems in Argentina. Figure 2.2 and Table 2.2 show the numbers of adults who registered on Welsh courses in Patagonia between 1997 and 2005. In April 2001, a three-week training course for tutors and other interested parties was conducted in Patagonia by Helen Prosser, the former director of the Centre for Teaching Welsh to Adults

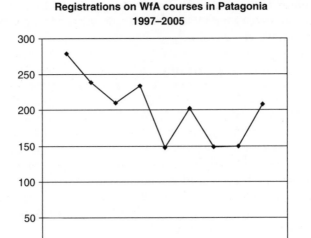

Figure 2.2 Registrations on WfA courses in Patagonia (*Source*: Welsh Language Project 2005 Annual Report)

Table 2.2 Registrations on WfA courses in Patagonia

Year	Total registrations	Year	Total registrations
1997	279	2002	202
1998	239	2003	149
1999	210	2004	150
2000	234	2005	208
2001	148		

in Cardiff, to ensure sufficient local people are available to help the tutors from Wales and able to take over should this become necessary in the future (Prosser, 2001).

Intensive language learning

From 1974, adult provision for Welsh learners took two main forms: intensive courses and classes attended on a weekly basis, initially mainly in the evenings. Intensive courses in Welsh were based on the ULPAN model developed in Israel in 1949 from the teaching methods used in the 1880s by Eliezer Ben-Yehuda whose vision and diligence revived Hebrew as a spoken language.

There was considerable interest in Wales in emulating Israel's example in the 1960s and early 1970s (Evans, 1969; Garlick, 1968; Maro, 1971). In 1972, Shoshana Eytan of the Education Department of the International Jewish Institute spoke in Cardiff about her experience of the Hebrew ULPANIM. The following year, Gwilym Roberts and Chris Rees, pioneers in Welsh language teaching inspired by her lecture, began the first ULPAN course in Cardiff (G. Roberts, 1994), renamed 'WLPAN' in order to sound more Welsh. The group met five times a week and were taught by a team of volunteer tutors. Eleven students began the 100-hour course and ten completed. Gwilym Roberts, an experienced tutor, described the results as 'staggering' as students learned as much in 10 weeks as people would normally learn in two years of weekly lessons (Newcombe, 1995; Osmond, 1973: 11).

By 1982, there were 43 WLPAN courses in Wales. Courses varied in intensity: classes were held at least three and, in some cases, four or five times per week either during the day or in the evening, for at least 100 hours. The expansion of Welsh-medium education for young children during the same period inspired many adults to learn Welsh and, often, students attending WLPANIM were parents of young children attending Welsh-medium nursery schools (R.O. Jones, 1999: 446). As the intensive provision grew, so did more advanced courses to follow the WLPANIM on both an intensive and a weekly basis. Over the same period, weekend and week-long residential courses also took off.

In Summer 1980, an eight-week residential WLPAN course at Lampeter, West Wales, attracted approximately 40 students; it now accommodates over 60 students each year. Students, presented with 3000 to 3500 items of active vocabulary are able to hold a conversation about everyday activities at the end of the 400-hour course. Regular social events reinforce the language presented in the classroom; native speakers are invited to speak to students in class on weekends; and students are expected to practise in the local community. The course was nicknamed 'Welsh with tears' (Rees, 2000) because of the effort students need to expend; one of the participants on the 2001 course was heard to comment that her brain was hurting because of the intensity (Jones-Williams, 2002).

The 1980s and 1990s were a time of continuing expansion of provision. The drop-out rate for WLPAN is low and compares favourably with statistics for language classes in England and Wales (WJEC, 1992: 7–9, 24). The availability of these intensive courses is the main factor that differentiates the current teaching of WfA from teaching foreign languages to adults in Wales. An intensive course or some immersion element generally figures in the successful Welsh learner's experience (see, for instance, A. Evans, 2004; Gillibrand, 1992; Gruffudd, 1980; Preston, 1997; S. Thomas, 2001; Trosset, 1984). I. Jones (Gruffudd, 1980), for instance, had accumulated a great knowledge of Welsh from books but only became a confident speaker after attending an intensive course. Kinney (1992: 2) also reports a dramatic change after attending a two-week intensive course: 'It is perfectly true to say that I went in an English speaker and came out two weeks later speaking Welsh. Imperfect, halting and full of mistakes – but Welsh'. Subsequently Kinney pursued a distinguished career in broadcasting through the medium of Welsh. Ryder (Unidentified, 1998a) also attained a high degree of fluency after learning Welsh on an WLPAN, a skill which may have contributed to her election as mayor of Ruthin in 1998 and subsequently as a member of the Welsh Assembly Government.

The success of these initiatives was such that provision for more advanced students also needed to expand, with opportunities for fluent learners to join native speakers on advanced courses such as *Gloywi Iaith* [polishing language], *Cymraeg Busnes* [Business Welsh] and various literature and translation courses. These accredited courses can contribute to a certificate or a BA in Welsh. Alternatively, students can register for degree courses in Welsh for second language speakers. Aberystwyth University also provides a distance learning degree programme in Welsh, which is open to advanced learners.

By the 1990s, the psychological barriers which discouraged adults from learning the language had finally been broken down (WJEC, 1992). Welsh was not only a language that could be learned in adulthood, but the success of adult learners in Wales had the potential to inspire language learners elsewhere.

Other Adult Provision

Intensive courses co-exist with a range of other classes for adults, now co-ordinated by the WfA consortia and mainly funded by the National Council, ELWa. Provision is divided between educational establishments on a local basis. Higher education institutions are responsible for intensive learning (over four contact hours per week), whereas further education organisations and other organisations such as the Workers' Education Association (WEA) and voluntary bodies provide weekly classes. Some voluntary bodies run intensive courses but these generally have fewer contact hours than those run by higher education establishments. Courses are arranged by individual providers, but the programme for the whole area is organised by the local WfA Consortium. In 1994, eight WfA Consortia, coterminous with the old counties of Wales, were set up to co-ordinate provision (Prosser, 1995, 1996, 1996/1997). The consortia consist of WfA providers from universities, higher and further education colleges, some unitary authorities and the WEA. The role of the consortia is joint planning of programmes to ensure full provision in each area and to avoid duplication. Each consortium produces a publicity booklet listing all courses. Prior to 1995, different providers used different names to describe courses of the same level. Whilst this practice still exists, each course now also includes a national 'stage' descriptor.

After the passing of the 1993 Welsh Language Act, which requires that all public bodies give equal status to Welsh and English, 'Welsh-in-the-workplace' courses increased quite rapidly in number and continue to be an increasingly important element of WfA provision. Workplace ventures have enjoyed a varied degree of success as these pioneering initiatives have generated some problems, which I will discuss in Chapter 7. However, even in the short interval since the AWLP data was collected, workplace courses have expanded both in number and intensity, many enjoying a great measure of success. At the National Eisteddfod in 2006, for instance, *Canolfan Byd Gwaith* [Job Centre Plus][1] presented awards to four workplace learners recognising their outstanding progress in Welsh language skills and use of Welsh in the workplace. Some employers have been particularly proactive. Helen Prosser (2003) comments on the commitment of a South Wales bank to producing bilingual employees. Similarly, Gwynedd Council have recognised the hard work of staff in this area since 1999 by awarding two prizes annually, one for those who have made the most progress over a 12 month period and one for those who have 'crossed the bridge' from an L2 learner to L2 speaker in a 12 month period.

In 1998, the Welsh Language Board assumed responsibility for co-ordination of the WfA work with special emphasis on nationwide strategic planning. An officer was employed with a remit for WfA work and, on the basis of recommendations in *Making Wales a Bilingual Nation* (E.W. Thomas, 2001), the National Council, ELWa, established a new unit which assumed responsibility for the development and promotion of WfA and post-16 education in 2002. WfA has two main aims: to increase the numbers of Welsh-speakers in the community and the workplace and to enable people to learn other subjects through Welsh. There are two further subsidiary aims: the first is to improve the fluency of students, including beginners, intermediate learners, and good learners who are attending advanced classes in order to learn how to use Welsh in the workplace – the intention, then, is to close the gap between learners and fluent speakers;

the second aim is to highlight the economic advantages of speaking the language in order to extend participation and increase demand, establishing a pattern of creating and then fulfilling the need for Welsh lessons. ELWa has responsibility for strengthening the programme of WfA throughout the country and, in so doing, ensuring opportunities for people to develop bilingual skills.

Within this framework, a number of initiatives offer invaluable support for adult learners.

Cyd (Together)

Cyd organises a wide range of activities aimed at bringing learners and fluent speakers together in an informal and social environment. Most activities are arranged through a network of branches throughout Wales (and several outside) supported by *Cyd's* paid staff. Activities include coffee mornings, pub sessions, quizzes, concerts, talks, walks, dances and weekends away. A key part of the programme is the *Cynllun Pontio* [Bridging Scheme] whereby native speakers attend classes on a rota basis to give learners semi-naturalistic language practice.

Nant Gwrtheyrn Welsh Language and Heritage Centre (Y Nant)

Y Nant, situated in a particularly scenic part of North West Wales, is an important centre for WfA learners inside and outside Wales. Many learners claim that they progressed from learner to fluent speaker as a result of their time there. This remote village of 26 houses was bought by a trust established by Carl Clowes, a medical doctor and Welsh learner, in 1978. Since its renovation, hundreds of people, families or individuals, have visited each year (Clowes, 1992; Gwynedd, 1999; Rhys, 1987). The aim of the tutors at Nant Gwrtheyrn is to teach Welsh in a relaxed and fun-filled manner. They offer total immersion courses for students cut off from influences from the outside world, such as television or radio. For one afternoon, students are taken to real-life situations to practise what they have learned with people who use the language naturally on a day-to-day basis (Pugh, 2005; Unidentified, 2001).

Literature and media provision for Welsh learners

As the numbers of learners increased, so did the need for course material for adult learners. A great deal of reading material specifically aimed at learners has been produced over the years in a wide variety of genres, from 'chick lit' to poetry to a novel for learners about the adventures of a group of learners on a residential course (Clayton, 1996). A magazine for learners, *Lingo Newydd*, is produced 6 times a year. Television and radio provision for learners has also expanded since the early 1990s (for more details see Newcombe, 2002c) and Welsh learners have featured regularly on programmes undertaking challenges to use the language in the community. There have even been Welsh learner reality television programmes in which members of the public and celebrities from the world of sport, journalism and drama have participated. Some learners, unable to attend courses regularly because of work and family commitments, rely on Welsh language programmes, including those for young children, to help them extend their knowledge (Devine, 2005). Some of the programmes created by *Acen*[2] are set in the workplace, reflecting the increasing awareness of using Welsh in new domains. Gaelic and Irish series inspired by *Acen's Now You're Talking* with attendant course materials have proved popular in Scotland and Ireland. Figure 2.3 outlines the milestones in WfA provision.

- First edition of *Cymraeg i Oedolion* [Welsh for Adults textbook] using *Cymraeg Byw* [Living Welsh: see p.28] published (1963);
- The first WLPAN course in Cardiff (1973);
- Cardiff University Centre for teaching Welsh to adults opens (1975);
- *S4C* [Channel 4 Wales] provides Welsh Language programmes (1982);
- The Welsh Language Board established (1988);
- The Welsh Language Act (1993) requires that public bodies make provision to use Welsh and English equally;
- Eight consortia are established for WfA in the old county areas of Wales (1994);
- The Welsh Language Board assumes responsibility for co-ordination of the WfA work with special emphasis on nationwide strategic planning (1998);
- The National Council, ELWa establishes a new unit which assumes responsibility for developing and promoting WfA and post-16 education (2002);
- The National Council, ELWa announces plans to reform WfA and extend provision (2004/5);
- Six further and higher education institutions selected to become dedicated language centres to plan and deliver WfA provision (2006).

Figure 2.3 Significant milestones in WfA provision

Plans for Reforming WfA

Despite the greatly increased interest in the language, provision and resources are insufficient to provide the professional service that many centrally involved in the WfA field seek to provide. For instance, Prosser (2004) argues that more financial resources would make it possible to employ full-time tutors, leading to greater security and professionalism. Higher levels of funding would also make it possible to harness the enthusiasm and motivation of beginners by providing support for their efforts to use the language outside the safety of the classroom.

ELWa is currently considering proposals for a wide-ranging review which builds upon what has been achieved through:

- better planning and marketing of courses to identify and target potential learners.
- far more full-time career tutors, giving the whole programme a more professional outlook.
- clearer progression routes allowing learners to achieve fluency more rapidly.

According to the head of the Bilingual Learning Unit at ELWa, Ann Jenkins: 'The time has come to move this hugely important programme into the mainstream of education with all the resources, backing and co-ordinated planning and funding it needs to achieve its task' (Rees, 2004: 32).

The launch of the *Cyfrwng* [Medium] Project in 2005 represents an important step towards achieving these aims. Developed in response to NAfW's agenda to create a bilingual Wales, it cements the various facets of WfA. An important feature of this initiative is the WfA Information Line which directs every caller to the most suitable provision. It also provides programmes for various target groups, such as parents of children who attend Welsh-medium schools, those who have moved into Welsh speaking areas, and learners in the workplace. Each group will have the opportunity to network with organisations on a national and local level.

ELWa (2005) has also produced a booklet, *All you need to know about learning Welsh (but were too afraid to ask)*, with advice on choosing an appropriate course as well as details of courses online, useful websites and chat rooms, media provision, learning materials, learner support and activities in the community.

In May 2006, the Welsh Assembly Government (WAG) announced that six further and higher education centres were to become dedicated language centres to plan and deliver WfA. The centres will provide training and career progression opportunities for tutors, and offer learners improved support and advice with the overall aim of achieving higher levels of learners reaching fluency (on WWW at http://newydd.cymru.gov.uk/news/ pressreleasearchive/educationandskills/may2006educ/).

Language Learning Methodology

The remarkable growth in adults learning Welsh has been linked, in part at least, to the revolutionary changes in teaching strategies in the western world which encouraged oral rather than written work, enabling learners to communicate more easily with native speakers. The main goal of the communicative approach can be summed up in a term coined by Hymes (1972) as 'communicative competence'. Communicative competence deals with actual speech in actual situations. Students should be able to interact with other people and thus 'getting the message across' is far more important than accuracy. Students learn through interaction with others and, in so doing, develop strategies of communication. Baker and Prys Jones (1998: 677) sum up the main tenets of communicative language teaching as follows:

- Language is a system for conveying meaning.
- The primary purpose of language is interaction and communication.
- Language can be analysed in terms of its grammatical structures, but also according to categories of meaning as used in speech events.

The main skills fostered in the communicative approach are generally *oral*. However, it can also be adapted to students' needs should they wish to develop reading and writing skills. Baker and Prys Jones (1998) describe communicative language teaching as an approach rather than a method or teaching style. A strong communicative approach advocates that language is acquired through communication. Rather than using communicative techniques to reinforce language already learned, language itself is learned and developed through communication. A weak communicative approach – the approach taken in WfA – combines different teaching styles such as audio-lingual, structural and grammar translation with opportunities for the learners to engage in communicative activities.

A more sanguine attitude to errors in grammar and pronunciation is found in the communication approach rather than in, for instance, the traditional grammar-translation method. Errors are regarded not as a cause for concern and censure but as an inevitable consequence of experimenting and risk taking. Moreover, students must be allowed to make errors in order to develop their own models of the target language. It is possible for students to communicate well both in the classroom and naturalistic settings while still making errors. Various terms, including interlanguage (Selinker, 1972, 1992), interlingua and transitional competence (Corder, 1981), to refer to the developing competence of L2 learners from the beginner stages where ability is very limited to the stage of near native fluency. It can be argued that formal language teaching should approximate as closely as possible to the learning of a second language in an informal setting, where students are allowed to communicate in 'interlanguage' without fear of censure.

Brumfit and Roberts (1983: 86–7) suggest that the most discouraging feature of traditional language teaching in schools has been its negative 'often highly punitive' attitude to error. Learners' utterances were judged in terms of the linguistic capabilities of the more intellectual adult native speakers of the target language and any deviations regarded as evidence of failure. However, as Scovel (2000: 147) comments: 'Errors may be the demonstration of originality, creativity and intelligence. Any parrot can mimic the teacher'. The generous margin for error allowed by the 'communicative approach' is arguably one of the most liberating features for learners. Although the ultimate aim is perfection, the objective *en route* is successful communication. This philosophy inspired and continues to inform WfA teaching schemes (Emyr Davies, 2000).

Cymraeg Byw (Living Welsh)

The production of the first version of *Cymraeg Byw* in 1964 was arguably the watershed in the phenomenal growth of learners (Cennard Davies, 1980). *Cymraeg Byw* is an attempt to define the main features of standard spoken Welsh, that is, the form of the language that lies somewhere between conservative literary Welsh on the one hand and the local regional dialects on the other (Crystal, 2000). Traditionally, the variety of Welsh taught as a second language to both adults and children was of a literary nature, bearing little resemblance to the Welsh learners would hear spoken in the community. Public examinations laid little emphasis on oral skills and it was common for adults to have gained qualifications in the language and yet be unable to speak it (P. Davies, 1992). Learners sufficiently courageous to attempt to do so, were confronted with unfamiliar registers of language and a range of dialects. Dyfed (1979: 269) reflects on the experiences of mid-20th-century learners who sought to put their literary Welsh knowledge to practical use in the following terms:

> *It took time to become accustomed to the oral language. I understood the teacher in the class, cassettes and the news on the television, but I completely failed to understand [Welsh language] programmes and everyday language. From 'Teach*

Yourself Welsh' I learned literary Welsh, from the BBC I learned living Welsh and from the ordinary people I learned dialect Welsh.

Comments such as these made providers and tutors realise the urgent need for the learners to be taught to *speak* the Welsh language. As courses expanded in the 1960s and 1970s, articles on *Cymraeg Byw* proliferated and the communicative approach began to take root (see for example, James, 1971; R.M. Jones, 1962; O.G. Jones, 1962; Prosser, 1985).

Changes in pedagogy have necessarily entailed changes in assessment. In the 1980s, the Welsh Joint Education Committee's (WJEC) officer in charge of WfA set out communicative assessment objectives for adult learners. In 1991, the WJEC set up two special examinations for adult learners *Defnyddio'r Gymraeg* [Use of Welsh] and *Defnyddio'r Gymraeg Uwch* [Use of Welsh, Advanced] with greater emphasis on oral/aural communication than in the L2 examinations in the school setting. This emphasis reflects the underlying ethos of the whole WfA enterprise, namely the creation of new Welsh-speakers able to use their language at home, in the workplace, and the community and 70 per cent of marks are now allocated to speaking and listening (E. Hughes, 2005). A particularly useful exercise in the intermediate examination is the task given to each candidate of recording a short conversation with a native speaker. A similar task for a longer conversation is set for the advanced examination as well as 20 hours of project work in a Welsh language situation. In 2001, WJEC formally joined ALTE (Association of Language Testers in Europe) and examinations are being amended according to their recommendations, but retaining the emphasis on oral communication.

WLPAN

The methodology of the WLPAN courses discussed earlier in this chapter also merits attention. The two important principles underlying the original ULPAN courses are intensive scheduling and direct methodology – Hebrew through Hebrew, with very little grammatical explanation. As Schuchat (1990) points out, however, the most distinctive feature is the intensive approach to learning, which is 'not a method but merely a schedule that fosters and reinforces language learning'. All ULPAN courses stress oral communication, with mimicry playing a large part in the lessons, particularly in the early stages, though the tutor is allowed a good deal of freedom in the classroom and encouraged to make use of games, role play and dialogues. A typical programme in the 1970s consisted of teaching 1140 words over a period of three to five months on everyday talk and political terms for reading newspapers and listening to the radio (Polani, 1978).

The emphasis from the beginning, then, was on providing learners with sufficient language for everyday communication.

The approach used in the WLPAN places the same emphasis on acquiring a basic vocabulary which can be used in day-to-day communication. The classes also owed a great debt to Dodson's (1967) bilingual method and its emphasis on drilling, particularly in the early years (see G.W. Jones, 1993: 180; Newcombe, 1995: Appendix 3; Emyr Davies, 2000: 19 for examples of drills). Dodson distinguished between 'medium-orientated' activities directed towards the 'form' (that is, grammatical structure) and 'message-orientated' activities where learners concentrate on using the language to transact meanings that matter to them. Effective language learning, however, involves a constant interaction between these two kinds of activity: each is necessary and neither is sufficient in itself.

Whilst disagreements exist among theorists on how language is learned, there is now broad general agreement that foreign language learning requires the interplay of different levels of cognition. According to Hawkins (1996: 29): 'The consensus view now is that the two "levels" of learning, both the study of grammar and the use of communicative activities, interact and enrich each other and both have a proper role in the apprenticeship'. Chris Rees (1995), former director of the Cardiff Centre for Teaching Welsh to Adults, maintains that so many other activities have been included as tutors have sought new ideas from a variety of sources that Dodson would hardly recognise his method now. On intensive courses, where it is important to keep the concentration of learners, teaching the same linguistic material in several different ways by different tutors provides valuable reinforcement. There is a general consensus within WfA that different approaches are suited to the needs of different groups and individuals (B. Davies, 1995; Cennard Davies, 2001; Price, 2001; Rees, 1995; Rhys, 1995); This approach, then, is consistent with what has been widely advocated in language learning over several decades (see, for instance, Brown, 2000; Naiman *et al.*, 1996; Richardson, 1983; Stevick, 1989).

As an WLPAN course progresses (usually after about 15 contact hours), the direct method, Welsh through Welsh, is increasingly used. The degree to which some English is used varies according to tutors' views. Some adhere strictly to the target language whereas others take the view that sometimes it is acceptable to include some English for explanatory purposes. Details of a typical WLPAN class in Cardiff can be found in Newcombe (1995, 2002c) and Rees (2000).

An eclectic approach also characterises the weekly classes offered by a variety of providers. Tutors are free to choose their own emphasis, provided that oral communication is the main goal and the agreed topics for assessment are covered. Most Local Authority weekly classes have used the course books, *Dosbarth Nos* [Evening Class] I, II and III, which are currently being superseded by radically updated versions (Conlon & Davies, 2006; Meek, 2005; Stonelake & Davies, 2006). However, tutors generally draw material from a variety of other sources including the media (for further information about WfA classes at all levels, see C. Jones, 2000). Some Local Authorities also run non-assessed courses for learners who want to practise speaking and gain fluency but do not wish to be assessed. Such groups are usually called *Siop Siarad* or *Clwb Siarad* and meet for two hours on a weekly basis.

Despite the growth in adults learning Welsh, the drop-out rate remains a matter of concern. Evas (1999, 2001) has challenged current methods of teaching Welsh, maintaining that they are not student-friendly, create needless stress and produce wounded learners. He advocates instead methods he regards as brain friendly. These include:

- suggestopedia (Lozanov, 1979), which relies heavily on inducing a relaxed atmosphere in the classroom and endeavouring to accelerate the learning process by seeking to understand and exploit the non-conscious influences to which students are consciously responding;
- the silent way (Gattegno, 1972) in which students learn by probing and problem-solving and where the tutor, who supplies exercises to encourage their competence in the language, intervenes only when absolutely necessary;
- community language learning (Curran, 1972) which aims to create a genuinely warm and supportive community among the learners and to gradually wean them away from complete dependence on the teacher, who takes the role of counselor, to complete autonomy;
- the natural approach (Krashen & Terrell, 1983) which emphasises meaning rather than form and that learners be provided with comprehensible and relevant input; and
- total physical response (TPR), which places listening comprehension in a central position (Asher, 1986).

Evas' views are based on new understandings of the architecture of the human brain. Little research has been undertaken on the merits of these methods, although anecdotal accounts offer some support. Talfryn (2001), for instance, claims that when suggestopedia was introduced into his intensive classes in North East Wales the drop-out rate reduced, but argues that this method is only suitable for use on intensive courses.

It should be noted, however, that 'brain friendly' methods are regarded by some scholars with a degree of scepticism (see, for instance, Brown, 2000). One area of concern affects the suitability of these approaches for all learners. For instance, although minimisation of anxiety is one of the main aims, it is possible that these methods could increase anxiety for some students. The exclusive use of the target language advocated by the proponents of suggestopedia, for instance, can be threatening for beginners. The emphasis on physical activity in TPR could also increase anxiety amongst adults who may feel self-conscious when required to perform actions. Singing is a valuable way to learn vocabulary. However, my experience as a practitioner has demonstrated that while some students seize the opportunity, others feel extremely uncomfortable. The natural approach advocated by Krashen and Terrell (1983), where students answer 'yes' or 'no' initially and only speak when they feel ready, may minimise anxiety but also poses problems. The use of material requiring 'yes' or 'no' answers at an early stage may well be non-threatening for those learning English as an L2 but would not help reduce anxiety in the Welsh situation, where there is a very wide range of ways of answering in the positive and negative. However, the identification of problems of this kind does not preclude experimenting with techniques associated with these methods (Brown, 2000).

Student views on methodology are illuminating. Adult learners often express positive views about drilling (James, 1974a; Newcombe, 1995; J.J. Williams, 1994). It can be argued, however, that the function of the classroom is not merely to teach language but to help build confidence to use language outside the classroom and this can only be achieved by participation in more authentic activities. Although this is an under-researched area, there are indications that students feel positively about the methodology used in WfA classes (Hedges, 2005; Lewis, 2001; Newcombe, 1995, 2002c), attributing their dissatisfaction instead to factors such as placement at an inappropriate level for their ability or insufficient written work for their needs.

In the absence of systematic evaluation of current WfA methodologies, it would seem expedient to continue to utilise an eclectic approach. A broad communicative approach embracing many methods within a flexible framework allows teachers to respond effectively to different learner needs. Although firm conclusions on methodology cannot be reached, WfA has achieved a great measure of success, all the more remarkable in an area traditionally regarded as 'the poor cousin' of the education system, dependent to a degree on the goodwill of volunteers.

Provision in Wales has been an inspiration to others. For instance, in 1994 eight tutors and administrators involved in the teaching of Gaelic made a study visit to South Wales where they observed courses at Carmarthen, Swansea, Pontypridd and Cardiff as well as visiting branches of *CYD* and a language centre in Swansea. They were impressed by the effectiveness of 'the rote-like attitude' on the intensive courses and the fact that very little English was used (Comunn Na Gaidhlig, 1994) and have patterned some courses on the Welsh experience.

Consolidating Learning in the Community

Irrespective of the success of adult learning provision in producing Welsh-speakers in the classroom, it is salutary to remember that even highly motivated students will rapidly lose skills which are not fostered after course completion. Some students can use their newly acquired skills with family and/or friends but, for those who have no such opportunities, practice in the community is vital. Although a great deal can be learned in the classroom, from private study, reading, the internet, and the media, it is only by using language acquired in this way with native speakers that speech is likely to become more spontaneous and natural. This poses a range of problems for adult learners in Wales. As Prosser (1997) points out:

> The field of teaching Welsh to Adults has shown that it is possible to learn the language. The creation of a nation of people who *can* speak Welsh is within our reach, but we have to go a stage further and create a nation of people who *use* the language.

This view is echoed by James (1998):

> *There is no shortage of Welsh-speakers but there is a shortage of Welsh users. Voices on the phone too ready to turn to English, colleagues in offices too busy, shop workers unaware of the treasure they have at their disposal, if only to offer the opportunity to customers to ask for a loaf of bread or a pound of potatoes in Welsh. When you think of the myriad of insignificant circumstances, day after day where simple language could be used to give a chance to these learners. Simple phrases that we repeat over and over daily. In everyday situations like this a relationship is created and nurtured and from this comes the confidence and satisfaction for learners and native Welsh-speakers.*

Lack of opportunity is not the only obstacle. Fear is a big stumbling block, even for those in the West and North where Welsh is still used on a regular basis in the community. For instance, Mary Burdett-Jones (2002), who works and lives in West Wales, tells how she lacked the confidence to converse in Welsh for 20 years despite having gained a first class honours degree in the language. In a similar vein, a NIACE study (Aldridge, 2001) reports that only 3 out of 33 respondents who said they spoke Welsh as a second language responded that they could join in a friendly informed conversation without difficulty. Use of language in the community, then, does not necessarily follow on from communicative competence in class. Factors such as learners' lack of confidence, availability of Welsh-speakers and difficulties in understanding contribute to learners' failure to reproduce their skills away from the relative safety of the classroom. The widespread view that using Welsh in new domains such as the workplace is an unrealistic aspiration for second language speakers can also be a stumbling block.

As the number of learners increased in the 1970s, so did the realisation of the need to integrate them socially and culturally into Welsh life, and to provide an opportunity to practise new linguistic skills. If students are to attain fluency, they need to use their language skills outside the classroom. For effective L2 teaching, there must be active use in 'authentic contexts', for as Krashen and Terrel (1983: 1) have emphasised, the purpose of language instruction is to allow the learner to 'understand language outside the classroom', so that ultimately he or she can 'utilise the real world, as well as the classroom'. Pegrum (2000: 4) makes a similar point:

> We should definitely begin this process at lower levels, and expand it as students advance in their learning. The bridges built between the classroom and the outside world, and the more gradual transition to 'post-classroom experience', will not only make language study more meaningful and motivating, but will stand the students in good stead when it comes time for them to go forth as completely independent learners, without the support of teachers, classmates or a language classroom.

A 1976 Welsh Office report on adult Welsh learners noted that, with the best intentions, Welsh-speakers may turn to English in the mistaken belief that they are displaying kindness. In the process, some may make it obvious, thoughtlessly or unintentionally, that the learner's Welsh is halting and slow. One of the recommendations of the report was for a campaign to persuade Welsh-speakers throughout the country to play an understanding and helpful part in supporting those of all ages who are learning the language. Suggestions included a badge to be worn by those willing to converse with learners and notices in places where there would be opportunities for them to practise. Attention was drawn to the fundamental need to awaken the awareness of Welsh-speakers to the growing importance of the learner in the struggle to strengthen the language, particularly in the more Anglicised areas where there are fewer opportunities to use the language in daily life. It was suggested that learners visit Welsh-speaking areas and that friendships with Welsh-speaking families in their own locality be arranged. It was also recommended that new clubs, specifically for learners, be established where Welsh could be used at a level appropriate to their needs and that Welsh-speaking organisations such as *Merched y Wawr* [Women of the Dawn], (a Welsh-speaking society for women, similar to the Women's Institute in the rest of the United Kingdom) provide assistance for learners. Biographical accounts of learners in the society's magazine *Y Wawr* testify in fact to the help learners have received outside classroom from members of *Merched Y Wawr*.

In 1972, *Pabell y Dysgwyr* [The Learners' Tent], renamed *Maes D* [Field D] in 2005, made its first appearance at the National Eisteddfod. Workers organise entertainment for learners, and there is a café area where learners can sit and converse. Competitions specifically aimed at learners are arranged, including one to identify the 'Learner of the Year'. The Learner of the Year award is presented annually to a learner who speaks well and is making a contribution to promoting Welsh in the community. Dan Lynn James (1974b), a pioneering and influential tutor of WfA, argued that Eisteddfod activities for learners should be widely advertised and an effort should be made to educate Welsh-speakers on how to help learners. He believed it was of vital importance to warn learners not to be deterred by comments such as: 'But we don't say it that way!' He also stressed that Welsh-speakers should be trained to respond sensitively to learners' faltering attempts. Cennard Davies (1978) and Gruffudd (1979) also encouraged learners to use their Welsh outside class during the same period. In addition, societies such as *Cyd, Merched y Wawr, Urdd Gobaith Cymru*, as well as local Welsh societies, have also been attempting to integrate learners into the community for many years.

However, the integration issue is one that still requires urgent attention as will become increasingly clear in subsequent chapters. Prosser (2004), an influential tutor organizer in WfA stresses that it is vital to integrate learners into networks of fluent Welsh-speakers rather than keep them in learners' groups and stresses that, despite many valiant attempts, integration remains a major stumbling block, particularly in Anglicised areas such as south east Wales. This is a point to which I will return in subsequent chapters.

A report by the Welsh Consumer Council (WCC) in 2005 raises similar concerns about the extent to which the majority of adult learners use Welsh outside the classroom. It attributes the tendency to stay within the learner environment, only speaking to fellow learners and attending learner events, to a lack of both confidence and opportunity. Findings of this nature point clearly to the need for adult learners to be supported in their attempt to use the target language in the community.

Conclusion

Welsh language learning for adults is flourishing. Never have so many adults been learning the language formally in Wales and never has there been so much interest outside the country. However, adult learners differ in many ways from child learners. Although they usually learn of their own volition and begin with high levels of motivation, the responsibilities of adult life and the anxiety about their performance before their peers, particularly with regard to oral language skills, may make it difficult to sustain their motivation to speak a second language.

Learning a language is one issue: using it is another. The Government inspectorate draws attention to the importance of maximising the success of Welsh for Adults provision if the target of five percentage points for growth by 2011 is to be achieved (Estyn, 2004). However, if this objective is to be achieved, growing importance will need to be attached to supporting second language learners 'to cross the bridge' (Davies, 1973; Morris, 2001) to becoming second language speakers. In the following chapters, the focus will be on identifying specific barriers to progress and ways in which these can be addressed.

Notes

1. An agency which provides help and advice on jobs and training for people who can work and financial help for those who cannot.
2. Acen is a limited company providing courses for learners in the workplace and on-line and produces resources for learners in the form of books, CDs, videos and DVDs.

Chapter 3

The Learner's Experience in the Community

The first big breakthrough in learning the language comes, not when you achieve near perfection in a formal class but when the locals continue to speak Welsh in your presence.

N. Jones (1989: 11), a learner from Ireland.

The burning question is what happens after the course ends? Do these learners remain as learners, or can they be successfully integrated into the mainstream of Welsh-language social networks? This is a bridge that needs to be crossed. Head knowledge and linguistic facility need to be translated into social reality. Learners need to be able to use their newly acquired skills, not just with their fellow learners and teachers but with other Welsh-speakers in a cross-section of normal everyday social contexts. Welsh has to cease to be a classroom language, and adult learners need to gain confidence in using it.

R.O. Jones (1999: 449).

Introduction

As discussed in Chapter 2, the phenomenal growth of WfA means that there are no shortage of opportunities for the formal study of the language: the challenge for those who take advantage of these opportunities is then to put their newly acquired knowledge into practice. The focus of the present chapter, therefore, is on barriers adult students of Welsh experience as they attempt to consolidate their learning in the community. It draws on auto-biographical and biographical accounts of learners and data from the Adult Welsh Learners' Project (AWLP), including journal entries, interviews and focus group discussion.

A growing body of research points to the importance of this previously neglected area of language learning. Early positive encounters with native speakers are now widely recognised as pivotal in learners' development of skills, confidence, self-reliance, and feeling of integration (Lamping & Ball, 1996; Oxford, 1990). Clément and Gardner (2001) similarly stress that context can have a profound effect on second language acquisition (SLA). Norton and Toohey (2001) advocate research approaches that focus not only on learners' internal characteristics, learning strategies, or linguistic outputs but also on the reception of their actions in particular socio-cultural communities. They argue that insufficient attention has been given by researchers to the 'power of social interaction', and that learners who are able to negotiate entry into the social networks of the target language are likely to become successful learners. MacIntyre *et al.* (2001), too, discuss the effect of social support on 'willingness to communicate' (WTC), the ultimate goal in L2 instruction. The following biographical accounts of Welsh learners add considerable weight to findings of this kind.

Beyond the Classroom

Learning it
you're safe enough
but don't give up
the worst
is still to come
seven years in night class
once a week wearing
the teachers down
your malice was all in the
switch from classroom
drills to breathless
chattering on the
Winter streets – *speaking*
it took courage.

(Greenslade, 1992: 20) [italics added]

When individual language learners move from the class into the wider community they often experience 'language shock', the frustration and mental anguish that results in being reduced to the level of a two-year-old in one's ability to communicate, and a phenomenon to which I will return in Chapter 5 (Schumann, 1986). There was certainly an awareness of the vast difference between the classroom and the real world among the AWLP students. Alan commented in his journal: 'The *bwlch* [gap] is great'. Kim explained why: learners felt more secure in the classroom setting because *'in the classroom people speak clearly'*. She also commented that the tutor was paid to help and be patient whereas out in the community people were getting on with their lives and there was little awareness of learners' needs. She felt her attempts at speaking could be wearing on native speakers and recalled experiences with second language English speakers that she had found trying:

> 15 years ago I worked in the States (...). One of my fellow workers was a Japanese man with very little English. Another was an Italian woman who, although her English was quite good, had an incredibly strong Italian accent and a peculiar way of saying English words that made her very difficult to understand. I can remember some tortured conversations with one or both of them, wishing just for some peace and quiet! I can't help but think of these people sometimes when I'm speaking Welsh to people – I'm conscious that I may be making them suffer in the same way!

However, most students realise that the key to fluency is transferring skills acquired in class into real life situations. Neil Pfeiffer (2004) speaks for many when he writes: 'My Welsh was however, by and large, a matter of the classroom. The next stage was to take it into the community'. Neil stresses the importance of perseverance: 'How easy it is to let it slip; for days to pass without thinking or speaking in Welsh'.

In the early stages, access to as few as one or two native speakers outside the classroom may be sufficient (Cennard Davies, 2000; Davies, 2006; Layland, 2001). R.S. Thomas, the much revered poet, for instance, was greatly helped by Rev. H.D. Owen in Manafon, Mid-Wales:

> Almost every week through all weathers he would walk to the home of H.D. having done his homework. (...) He was given a warm welcome by H.D. and his wife, Megan in their home, and after struggling on for years at their expense he came to speak Welsh quite satisfactorily, although it took a long time, as he did not wish to impose on these kind people too often. (Thomas, 1997: 51, 55).

Like Kim, he was aware that it was an effort for his mentors to encourage him in his speaking efforts.

Four main issues emerge in learners' accounts of their attempt to use Welsh in the community: the tendency for native speakers to switch to English, code switching and code mixing, the speed of speech, and dialect differences.

Language Switching

One of the main problems for learners seeking to practise outside the classroom is persuading native speakers to maintain a conversation in Welsh. Autobiographical and biographical accounts of learners in journals in the 1970s and 1980s indicate that the opportunity for practice was limited. Such accounts proliferated in this period as the number of learners grew rapidly and the emphasis shifted from grammar translation to communication (see Jones & Newcombe, 2002; Prosser, 1985). Brown (1971: 39), like many learners during this period, experienced problems convincing Welsh-speakers that he could hold a conversation in Welsh. Whilst they would willingly exchange greetings and a simple comment on the weather, they switched to English in order to communicate on other topics. He maintained that 'the unwelcoming attitude was widespread and possibly typical'. Similarly Jacobs (1976: 14) wrote: 'In Wales, the language for speaking to strangers is English', a practice he interpreted as a kind of courtesy. Jacobs was living in an area where Welsh was the language of day-to-day activities. However, he recognised that learners' problems are even greater where Welsh is not the medium of daily communication but believes these can be overcome 'by a deliberate ideological commitment to the cause of the language'.

Even in the 1990s, when learners were rapidly increasing in numbers, there are many reports outlining the difficulties experienced by learners in persuading native speakers to hold conversations in Welsh. According to R.O. Jones (1999), the general tendency is to turn to English when one hears faltering Welsh from a struggling speaker. Participants in the AWLP confirm this to be the case. Kim, for instance, expressed her disappointment at this pattern of response: 'Sometimes people do not wait until I have found the word. They try to help me – they turn to English – aargh!' Alan expressed similar feelings of rejection and frustration:

> You put yourself on the line, there's no shield, if they reject you on language you're rejected, not really taken seriously, condescended to. As if they're saying, 'Speak English, it's much nicer for both of us'. It's demoralising and I wonder why do I bother?

Lewis (1999: 119) comments that many of her students have noted such problems.

> They can get exercises right when nothing depends on it, but when a whole lot of factors come into play in a real conversation then things are not so easy. The time factor is crucial. Most people want to finish a sentence in reasonable time, especially when someone is waiting to hear it. The ideas move faster than the language and, of course, you are taking

part in a dialogue, not making a speech, so the other person's contributions have to be taken into account.

The more advanced the AWLP students, the more they were troubled by native speakers switching to English. When students are close to fluency, they are likely to feel that the native speaker is making a judgment not only about their linguistic skills but also about their acceptance within the target community, an issue that will be discussed further in Chapter 4.

It might be assumed that it is easier for learners to practise the language in the Welsh heartland areas of North West and West Wales. However, this is not always the case. Alison Layland (2001), Welsh Learner of the Year in 1999, who lives in such an area, reports that she experienced ongoing difficulties in persuading some local people to use Welsh with her for day-to-day activities.

The reluctance of native speakers to sustain conversations in Welsh with learners is even evident in Welsh-medium nurseries where there is a tendency for learners and Welsh-speakers to form separate groups, with any communication mediated through English. Lydia, an intermediate student, reported in her dialogue journal:

At *Ti a Fi* [Mother and Toddler] you tend to get two main groups, one of which is made up of Welsh learners and the other of native Welsh-speakers and, although I do try and interact with both groups, my ability to converse with native speakers is limited and they do not seem very good at accommodating me. In fact, quite surprisingly, they seem happier to speak to me in English than Welsh (unless this has something to do with my pained expression).

Sharon, another intermediate student, was equally discouraged at the response to her attempts to speak Welsh:

It was my turn to be the parent on duty at *Ysgol Feithrin* [Nursery School]. I asked the leader not to translate into English for me as my understanding is better than my spontaneous conversation, but she kept forgetting, which was frustrating because I began to feel a bit alienated and could not summon up enough confidence to speak Welsh to her.

In response to these journal entries, I made three observation visits, one to an *Ysgol Feithrin* and two to *Ti a Fi* groups to study Welsh learners' and native speakers' interaction covertly. I told the leaders I wanted experience of young children learning as my teaching background included only adults and teenagers. Interestingly, the leader who kept translating for Sharon was in fact a fluent L2 Welsh-speaker who had clearly forgotten any struggles she may have experienced in her early years of learning. She spoke very little Welsh to Andrea and Sharon, the two learners who were volunteer helpers, even offering them drinks and distributing photos in English, a situation way within their linguistic ability and this despite the fact that both of them were speaking Welsh to the children the majority of the time. Fluent L2 speakers, then, may also require reminding of the needs of learners, in particular those learners who are crossing the bridge from learner to L2 speaker where sensitivity to language switch is often interpreted as a reflection on the learner's ability to sustain a conversation. Visits to the *Ti a Fi* groups also confirmed the validity of the observations made by the journal writers, as learners and native speakers tended to polarise. At the first group, I spoke to a native speaker who said she would always speak to Sharon in Welsh in future as she had come to understand the value of practice for learners. However, a few weeks later, when the same person attended the other *Ti a Fi* group she continued to speak English to the learners, including Sharon. When I reminded her that Sharon needed practice, she responded by saying that practising with children was best for learners and that reading children's books and watching videos also helped. However, Sharon had been doing this for many years and needed practice with adults to help develop her oral skills.

These problems are not, of course, unique to Welsh learners. Norton Pierce (1995) reports similar issues in the ESL context in Canada, while Perryman (2004) claims that there is such an emphasis on learning English in China, it is hard to find an educated person who is content to talk with a learner only in Chinese. In Catalonia, learners report that native speakers often switch to Spanish when they notice hesitation on the learner's part. For instance Camardons *et al.* (2005) report that a learner interviewed by a volunteer helper commented: 'I start speaking Catalan and when they see I'm struggling they immediately switch to Spanish, so I can never speak Catalan with anyone. You're the only person I can speak Catalan to'. The challenges for learners of lesser-used languages are particularly daunting. MacCaluim (2000: 7) describes how difficult it can be for Gaelic learners in Scotland to be accepted seriously:

> Many learners feel themselves to be on the fringe of the Gaelic world of which they would dearly love to be part, due to negative experiences with native speakers who have refused to answer them in Gaelic or who have rudely asked 'What kind of Gaelic is that?' or who have expressed negative views about Gaelic. (This is not to say, of course, that most native speakers are like that!).

Questionnaire responses from learners also indicate that lack of encouragement from the Gaelic community was a major stumbling block to progress (Comunn Na Gaidhlig, 1992: 39). A similar phenomenon occurs in the Basque country (Perales, 2003). Reasons for both native speakers' and learners' reluctance to sustain interactions in Welsh are explored below.

Reasons for native speaker reluctance

The reasons for the reluctance of some native speakers to sustain conversations in Welsh are many and varied. One issue which has attracted a great deal of comment is native speaker insecurity about their own proficiency in the language. Gruffudd (1979), for instance, makes the point that many native speakers attended English-medium schools and did not have formal Welsh lessons; when they hear learners using words unfamiliar to them, they may well experience feelings of inferiority. Dafis (1985), Trosset (1993) and N. Jones (1993) also perceive Welsh-speakers' reticence as a manifestation of lack of confidence in their ability to speak the language correctly. Similarly, Jane Hafren Beynon (2006) reports that in West Wales, where she seeks to encourage liaison between learners and Welsh-speakers, she encounters many people who say, '*My Welsh isn't good enough to use with learners*'. Native speakers have described learners' Welsh variously as '*so perfect*' (Greenwood, 1971), 'too posh' (Hill, 1987), 'too correct' (Trosset, 1993), 'too good' (N. Jones, 1993), commenting that they speak as a *siaradwr bwcwelsh* [book Welsh speaker] (Castle, 2002).

Lewis (2001) notes that, sometimes, native speakers in West Wales are anxious speaking to those who use scholarly language rather than the local dialect. Bowie (1993) observes that only the more educated were willing to speak Welsh to her in North West Wales, the less educated preferring to speak English. These observations may explain why fairly fluent students studied by Morris (2001) reported difficulty in finding opportunities to practise. This issue is crucial for learners, for an anxious interlocutor will deter all but the most confident of learners. Nor is the situation unique to Welsh. Dufon (1999), for instance, experienced similar problems to Trosset (1986) in persuading native speakers to use Javanese when she was learning. They always used Indonesian. She believes this behaviour can be attributed partly to the fact that many Javanese are afraid to make mistakes.

Welsh-speakers, particularly those with no educational background in Welsh, sometimes lack the confidence to use numbers in Welsh and often count and give dates in English, a phenomenon not unique to Wales, but common also in Malta, where conversations in Maltese are interspersed with English numbers and dates (Lewis, 1969: 105). However, this tendency does not inspire learners, sometimes reinforcing the notion that Welsh is unsuitable for use in the business world. This is a theme which will be explored further in Chapter 7.

Learners are occasionally aware of confidence issues for native speakers. According to R. Jones (2005), they noticed that Welsh-speakers sometimes seemed hesitant to talk to them as they perceived the learners as speaking 'proper' Welsh with an understanding of correct grammar and vocabulary. One student commented: 'When you speak to some Welsh-speakers they don't like speaking to learners. They are almost frightened that I might have a better standard of Welsh than them'. Another had encountered the notion of using posh Welsh, which is clearly quite prevalent amongst native Welsh-speakers: 'Welsh-speakers don't mix with us. Natives say we speak posh Welsh'. This experience mirrors that of participants in the AWLP. Kim, for instance, was surprised that her parents-in-law lacked confidence in their Welsh skills: '*They say that I speak 'posh' with more correct words than they do!*' Cathy, for her part, speculated that when Welsh-speaking parents from school remarked: 'It's much easier to be your friend in English', they were commenting not on her Welsh but on their own. She also wondered whether the tendency to switch to English with learners was related to anxiety over conveying the correct information, given that transactions can be easily misunderstood in an L2. This could be the case particularly in the business context as Welsh-speakers, as well as learners, grapple with new vocabulary in this domain.

Lewis (2001: 23) throws interesting light on the reactions of native speakers. On his return to West Wales after having lived abroad for many years, he attempted to use more erudite Welsh than he had been in the habit of using in the local community and several people he spoke to for the first time formed the impression he had learned Welsh. He drew the conclusion that by speaking 'pure' Welsh, an individual is immediately categorised as a Welsh learner, which may not make integration into the local community easier.

Negative attitudes to the language

Welsh-speakers' diffidence about their language skills may also be associated with the negative attitudes that speakers of lesser-used languages often hold about their mother tongue (R.M. Jones, 1974). Although Wales is becoming more confident about its place in the world and the value of its language (Worrall, 2001), long-held attitudes are extremely resistant to change. Learners, particularly those from outside Wales, still report that native speakers are surprised in their interest in a tongue as 'insignificant' as Welsh.

Renegotiation of the language of communication

On other occasions, reluctance to speak in Welsh is associated with a renegotiation of the language of communication. It can be difficult to change from English to Welsh in the case of an interlocutor who has previously used English. An entry in Alan's journal, for instance, reads:

> Huw and family came this morning. We mostly speak English which disappoints me but when you have a long friendship with someone it is difficult to relax and converse in a language you have only been learning for four years and you are in your forties!

Similarly, Kim indicated that she frequently had to choose between having 'a nice relationship' and Welsh language practice. Problems of this kind are greatly exacerbated when dealing with members of the family. Mervyn, for instance, uses Welsh regularly outside the home but rarely with his family. Similarly, Roger Fenton (2002) speaks Welsh confidently to many native speakers but needed several attempts before he eventually succeeded in conversing with his wife in Welsh. Kim wrote in similar terms: 'I find it hard to speak to my husband in Welsh because I knew him first in English'. Similarly, despite her fluency, Mairi Higham's in-laws in Cardiff always speak English to her, and the only member of the family who uses Welsh with her is Sioned Glyn, her sister-in-law who lives in North Wales. Sioned, for her part, commented, 'I have always spoken Welsh to Mairi from the very beginning but when I am in Cardiff I find it very strange because all my family turn to English' (Glyn, 2002). These reactions mirror Norton Pierce's (1995) observations: having investigated learners' investment, a concept akin to motivation, she concludes that learners often feel least comfortable in the environments in which they wish to invest. Others, including Beynon (2006), also comment on the difficulties of speaking to extended family members in Welsh after gaining fluency as an adult.

Children can be particularly unhelpful, exacerbating learners' hesitancy. Roger, in his journal for the AWLP, recorded that he was disappointed by his children's response to his efforts to speak Welsh:

> My children go to Welsh medium primary school and are regarded by my first language Welsh-speaking neighbours as being indistinguishable from first language Welsh-speakers. However, they [my children] find my attempts at speaking Welsh excruciatingly amusing but refuse to explain where I am going wrong. Conversations therefore last a few

minutes only before they collapse into English. With my exam coming up I have been promised more co-operation – we shall see. I suspect that they like having a language in which they can talk and which they think I cannot understand.

There is wisdom in Cathy's comment as part of focus group discussions, however: 'If you're very motivated you won't be too bothered about your family's response'. Motivation, possibly the key to overcoming so many hindrances to using an L2, will be discussed in more detail in Chapter 7.

Native speakers' expectations clearly play an important role. Alan comments:

Nan from North Wales is a first language Welsh-speaker. She *expects* me to speak Welsh, just as the staff at the nursery and school expect me to. At work I met up with Colin who used to be in my team. He is from Swansea and we always speak Welsh even though I struggle sometimes. It's this *expectation* bit again (. . .) I talked to the head teacher about Rick – now she never uses English. No, I can't remember a single occasion! Again, it is *her expectation* (. . .) I phoned Albert, who was a strong influence on my decision to learn Welsh. Again we have reached the point where *we expect* to speak Welsh together.

Sharon sensed that some children at nursery were not sure whether to speak Welsh to her or English but observed nonetheless that she found it easy to speak Welsh to one little girl as: She *expects* people to speak Welsh to her.

Accent

Accent may also play a part in language choice. Ball (1998) demonstrates a relationship between learner accent and the willingness of native speakers to use the Welsh language in communication. Hughes (2002) argues in a similar vein that, although learners can easily be forgiven for making syntactic errors, native speakers find a poor accent very difficult to tolerate. R. Roberts (2002) reports of instances when, as a schoolboy learning the language, he was ridiculed because of his accent lend support to this position. Six out of seven specialists interviewed by Hughes (2003) also made a connection between the learners' accent and the language switch. According to one, Elwyn Hughes, an experienced tutor / organiser, native speakers in North Wales were willing to speak Welsh with learners from South Wales with a Welsh accent and intonation but spoke English to those who spoke Welsh with an English accent. He believes that extrovert learners who are willing to imitate Welsh intonation are more likely to be accepted by Welsh-speakers than those who speak accurately but have an unfamiliar accent. Learners are often aware of the problems raised by accent. Several students interviewed by Davies (2006), for instance, indicated that they needed more help with listening work in class in order to make themselves more comprehensible to native speakers.

Interestingly, accent would not seem to be as crucial an issue in other settings. Perryman (2004), for instance, comments:

Fluency is very important in China – people will try to understand you if you talk fluently around what you are trying to say, even if you don't have the exact right word. Accent – which varies wildly across the vast land, seems less important.

Seriousness of intent

The fact that many learners aim not to attain fluency but to get by in the language complicates the situation still further. Emyr Davies (2005) argues that Welsh-speakers are more helpful if they realise that someone is serious in their effort to learn, and this understanding is often linked with the knowledge that a student is preparing for an examination, a phenomenon reported in relation to EFL learners in Japan (Kluge & Taylor, 2000). Furthermore, aims may change as learning progresses. Some students who initially only intended to acquire a smattering of the language opt to become fluent and be fully integrated into a Welsh community. Others choose only to 'get by', whereas their initial aim was fluency.

Conceptual difficulties

Trosset (1986: 172) puts forward the argument that: 'The real reason people do not speak Welsh to learners is that they have no real concept of a non-Welsh Welsh-speaker. They do not know, conceptually, what to do with learners, whether to treat them as Welsh or as English'. F. Roberts (2002), an experienced tutor and one of the instigators of the *Cynllun Pontio*, a scheme which offers learners opportunities to practice with native speakers, has observed in Aberystwyth that native speakers have a clearer understanding of learners' potential after involvement with the scheme. Many native speakers have admitted to her that they did not anticipate being able to hold lengthy conversations with learners before participating in *Cynllun Pontio*. Native speakers clearly need time to adjust to the growing number of learners, as well as advice on how to support them as they attempt to use the language in the community.

Reasons for learner reluctance

While the switch from Welsh to English is usually initiated by native speakers, learners also sometimes take this course of action. The omnipresence of English is such that learners need to be particularly determined to use the Welsh language. The situation is neatly summarized by Petro (1997: 3–4), a Welsh learner from the United States:

> The fact of the matter is that the principality of Wales is buried beneath the verbal tonnage of English (. . .) It takes fierceness and mental blinkers to learn it by pretending that you and the person with whom you're practising really don't share another language (. . .) Whenever I try to practise Welsh in Wales I get only so far before English comes spilling in from all sides.

Stress may also influence learner resolution. Tiredness was a factor for some participants in the AWLP, particularly for those with young children. Kim reported that she found it difficult to maintain L2 conversations when very tired. When a close relative had been diagnosed with a serious illness, Alan reported feeling low and debilitated when trying to use Welsh, and sometimes wondered why he ever made the effort. In a similar vein, N. Jones (1993: 161) reports the case of an English person living in rural Wales, who explained why he did not make the effort to learn Welsh in terms of the 'misfortunes' of other learners: 'I distinctly remember poor old Jonathan hunting down the Welsh-speakers in the coffee room, and having to nail them to the wall to get them to speak to him'.

Learners, of course, have the power to influence the behaviour of native speakers. Some of those interviewed by Newcombe (2002c) realised that they could, for instance, ask Welsh-speakers to repeat words and phrases they had not understood; they could also make a positive decision to persist in speaking in Welsh even when the Welsh-speaker switched to English. Some blamed themselves for their lack of persistence, which they attributed to their own laziness; they also indicated that they were both disappointed and relieved to return to English at the earliest opportunity. Such ambivalence was summed up by Petro (1997: 47) in the following terms: 'Every time one of us begins a sentence in English I wince under the twin reflexes of relief and shame'.

Positive experiences

Not all learners, however, report negative experiences. Gillibrand (1992), for instance, paid tribute to the people of Dolgellau who laboured to teach him Welsh, and a Welsh learner in rural Wales interviewed by Noragh Jones (1993: 129–130) maintained that she would never have spoken Welsh but for the support of local Welsh-speakers, especially the *Merched y Wawr*:

> They welcomed me to their meetings, even though for the first year I used to sit like a mouse, afraid to try out my Welsh among such experts. But I listened and finally I was able to understand what they were going on about, and then I did speak out, and they all turned round and looked at me, as if the cat had started to talk! (. . .) Without these women I would never have been able to do what I had to do – settle in the village, and improve my Welsh to the point where I could get a professional bilingual post, and make good friends (. . .)

Lynne Evans (1989: 26) is also positive about help from Welsh-speakers. She appealed for help from a Welsh-speaker when her efforts at learning through books, the Bible, and radio stalled: '*I received welcome, support and advice far beyond that for which I had hoped*'. In a similar vein, Lois Martin-Short (1998: 19) praises native Welsh-speakers who came to help learners at *Cyd*: '*Speaking is hard work for us but I know that it isn't easy to listen to learners and think of a simple way to express things*'. When Rosemary Jones (2006) moved from London to Cellifor, a small village in North East Wales, the support of local native speakers allowed her to become sufficiently proficient to teach technology through the medium of Welsh: '*From the beginning I received worthwhile help from neighbours and the mothers at the nursery school*'.

Sometimes situational demands override the reluctance of Welsh-speakers to assist learners. P. Thomas (2001: 21), when working as a vicar in a Welsh heartland area, was supported and helped by his parishioners, who sought to immerse him 'in a sea of Welsh'.

And, in spite of the disappointment reported by participants in the AWLP at the response of native speakers, not all experiences are negative. In addition to the frustration reported by Lydia, there were also memorable successes:

> This afternoon I took Emyr to Ti a Fi. I tried to speak as much Welsh to him as possible. One of the Welsh-speaking grandmothers came over and chatted a little bit to me. I tried to speak Welsh back and she said that she would always try to speak to me in Welsh so that I can practise.

Code Switching and Code Mixing

For the purposes of the present discussion, I make a distinction between the language switching described above, on the one hand, and code switching and mixing, on the other hand. Language switching concerns the behaviour of native speakers toward learners. It is motivated by the decision by either party to change from Welsh to English, though, in most cases, this decision is taken by the native speaker rather than the learner. There is therefore a clear dimension of power.

Code switching, in contrast, concerns the alternation between two or more languages in the course of discourse between people of comparable levels of competence in the two languages. It is a feature of normal conversation in stable bilingual communities, as witnessed in labels such as Denglisch (German and English) and Franglais (French and English) (Wyn, 2001). Code switching is usually intentional, and is triggered by factors such as situation, subject, or sense of belonging; it occurs at phrase or sentence level. In code mixing, a related phenomenon, people take words or short phrases from one language to another; this phenomenon is often unintentional. Although such patterns of language use are often highly stigmatised, there is no evidence to suggest that bilinguals are unable to separate the languages.

Code switching and code mixing are very much a part of Welsh-English bilinguals. Deuchar (2006) indicates that the majority of participants in a study of bilinguals in North Wales had Welsh as the matrix language and were able to use the full range of linguistic resources available to them. She concludes that this bodes well for the future co-existence of the Welsh language alongside English as the bilinguals compared well with members of other stable bilingual communities around the world.

While it can be argued that code switching presents opportunities for learners to conduct more extended and more natural conversations, notions of linguistic purity often lead them to perceive code switching as unhelpful. Higham (2002), for instance, appreciates that some natives speakers, particularly the elderly, do not feel comfortable using Welsh terminology for more recent concepts, such as electricity or computers, but expresses disapproval for code mixing such as *'On i'n really geto along gyda teacher cello fi'* [But I really get along with the cello teacher].

Laura was clearly grappling with this problem when she wrote in her journal:

> When I try to speak Welsh (which I don't do very often – still no confidence I'm afraid), people don't seem to understand me at first and I have to try again – it could just be that they are expecting me to speak English! Some people have said to me that it is daft to use 'proper Welsh' and told me I should use English words instead of the Welsh. Personally I think that, as a learner, I should try not to mix the two languages and that Welsh should be kept as pure as possible (if you know what I mean?!?). I actually find it

more difficult when people [codeswitch] as I get more lazy when I'm listening because you can get the gist of the conversation from all the English words!

Learners at focus groups also tended to disapprove of code switching and code mixing. Philip complained, for instance, that family members who were native speakers frequently used words such *'mantelpils'* for mantelpiece when a perfectly good Welsh expression *'silff ben tân'* was in common usage. Bilinguals, however, are unlikely to change such habits to accommodate learners, so learners need to adapt to this behaviour.

Speed of Natural Conversation

The speed of native speakers' speech is often a concern for second language learners. Perryman (2004), for instance, describes her own experience of learning English in China in the following terms:

> In China, because contact with foreigners and the outside world is limited, they often have trouble slowing down or simplifying the language to help a learner. Finding a language helper – or indeed a formal teacher in a university – who can do this, is worth its weight in gold.

Enfield (2003) also identifies speed as a problem faced by learners when they move from the 'idealised' language of the classroom into real life communication:

> Now it is my belief that the Linguaphone course never teaches the language it purports to teach, it teaches something else, which should be called a Lingua-language. Lingua-French and Lingua-German are, I am quite sure, different from the languages that they speak in France and Germany. They are a great deal nicer for a start. If you learn Lingua-English you would say, in carefully modulated tones, such things as 'Please may I have another one', whereas the native population say 'C'd ivor nuther' or possibly 'Gisser nuvver'. I therefore go about Greece asking carefully for another one, at which all the Greeks are greatly surprised, as they are gissernuvvering.

There is ample evidence that second language learners frequently encounter 'gissernuvvering' Welsh-speakers. In the WCC study (R. Jones, 2005), several students reported finding it difficult to keep up with native speakers who, like all fluent speakers, tended to speak faster than the tutor in class. One WCC student volunteered: 'They speak 'turbo' Welsh, it's hard to keep up'. Similarly, Agnes bemoaned the use of elisions: 'Modern Welsh is too abbreviated'. Laura complained that, while Welsh-speakers known to her spoke at an acceptable speed, she often found the pace of unfamiliar Welsh-speakers demoralising. Similarly, Rees indicated that some Welsh-speakers seemed oblivious of his limitations and spoke so fast that he rapidly became lost. According to Alan, 'They start slowly, but forget you're a learner and speed up'. Kim, for her part, was troubled that her young son spoke so quickly to her husband – a native speaker – that she frequently had to ask for a translation. Sharon, an intermediate student, observed that the rapid speech of native speakers sometimes resulted in unnecessary code switching. Welsh-speakers, in her opinion, needed to allow more time for the learner to work out what has been said and to formulate an answer. Philip reported similar experiences: he had found that, even though Welsh-speakers are supportive, they tend to speak speedily and at great length. As a result, he often loses the thread, another reason for both parties to switch to English. Agnes commented that speech was sometimes too fast for her even on television programmes for learners. Sioned wrote at length about the issue of speed in her journal:

> My friend came to visit from the North of England and we went to meet one of his friends. She automatically started to speak to me in Welsh so I said in Welsh that I was learning but I couldn't speak Welsh. She looked very surprised. I think when people hear my name they expect me to speak Welsh. In the evening she was speaking Welsh in front of us with her friends. (. . .) They were speaking quite quickly or it seemed they were speaking quickly. This is not the type of conversation where you can join in (. . .) It's much easier talking to a Welsh learner especially someone who is roughly on the same level as you because they don't expect too much of you and know how you feel when you are trying to speak Welsh, that is having to put in lots of bits of English and expecting to mess things up quite often. You're very willing to help one another out. Sometimes when you're speaking to a fluent Welsh-speaker you feel that they are getting impatient even when they are probably not and I quite often feel that they are expecting me to be better than I am. This is why sometimes if someone asks me something in Welsh I will answer in English because I don't want to let the other person down.

Interestingly, Sioned shows an emerging understanding that native speakers are not necessarily speaking particularly quickly or becoming impatient, and that much of the problem can be attributed to the fact that learners are straining to understand each word. This is a situation in which it is easy to apportion blame, but where an understanding of the needs of both groups is helpful. Although it is easier on one level, as Sioned realises, to practise with learners, this course of action is not conducive to language development. Learners cannot 'cross the bridge' to becoming second language speakers until they are able to communicate effectively with native speakers.

The speed of native speakers' speech can also be a problem for advanced learners. One such learner wrote in her diary about an opportunity to practise and discuss new developments in work, commenting: 'She speaks very quickly and it is still difficult for me to understand speakers like her'. It is very easy for Welsh-speakers to treat advanced learners as native speakers and to forget, or fail to realise, their limitations. Advanced learners, for their part, may feel more diffident to ask Welsh-speakers to reduce their speed of speech.

Dialect Differences

Accent has already been discussed in relation to the pronunciation of learners. For present purposes, the focus is on differences in dialect that affect morphology and lexis as well as phonology, and in relation to native speakers rather than learners. Dialect variation is a constant challenge for learners progressing from the standard language used in class to practising in the community. In settings such as Switzerland and in Arabic-speaking countries, educated speakers are able to switch between the 'high' variety used in more formal domains and the low variety used in domains such as conversation with family and friends (Ferguson, 1959; Fishman, 1967). In the case of speakers of lesser-used languages such as Welsh, however, it is the national language – in this case English – which alternates with regional varieties of Welsh; because Welsh has only been a medium of education for some segments of the population for the last few decades, many native speakers have a limited command of the standard language.

Dialect differences have implications for both learners and native speakers. Greenwood (1971: 64), for instance, raises the possibility that native speakers are put off by the more formal and literary Welsh of learners: she reports that some Welsh-speakers regarded her Welsh as 'so perfect'. In a similar vein, Roger Fenton (2002) reports that he and his wife would never speak more formal Welsh in front of their peers for fear of mockery. Kodesh (1982) discusses a similar phenomenon among Diaspora Jews who have learned Hebrew as a second language. Gruffudd (1980: 13) raises a related issue when he cites the observation of a Welsh learner called Pearse:

> Perhaps Welsh-speakers are too shy to reveal that they do not know some words that learners would know and it is a feeling of inferiority that causes them to switch to English.

Irrespective of the confidence of native speakers, dialect differences pose significant challenges for learners. Morris (1993: 9–10), for instance, records examples of learners' failed attempts to converse in Welsh when native speakers used sentence patterns which differed from the standard. Peter Boak (2005) sums up his own frustration in the following terms:

> It can be difficult, even after many years of knowledge of Welsh, to overcome a nervousness to use Welsh in all situations especially where you think only the local colloquial Welsh would be understood. I have a friend in North Pembrokeshire who is a Welsh-speaker and I can have difficulty following (and joining in) conversations using the local Welsh as there can be different vocabulary and pronunciation and quickness of speech.

Participants in the AWLP also identified this as a problem area. Kim, for instance, recorded: '*I feel fine speaking Welsh with people from the South and the West because my husband's family come from St. David's*'. She was disappointed, however, when a substitute tutor rebuked her for using this dialect in class. Her regular tutor, in contrast, encourages the students to use dialect as well as standard forms. Kim also complained:

> *I am unhappy speaking with North Walians. I think that it is a very, very different language! Sometimes, I think that I am improving and I will be fluent and then I hear North Walians in the street and think: 'Well, I didn't understand one word'.*

Rees, for his part, reported difficulties in understanding the dialects of North West Wales and West Wales and Lydia attributed problems understanding native speakers at nursery to their use of dialect. This situation poses a dilemma as to how much dialect should be included in courses. While some course material and examination papers are available in North and South Welsh versions, it is not feasible to include all dialect variations. Intensive courses vary considerably in the North, South and West of Wales but again do not cover all the dialectal versions of the patterns learnt. While frequently occurring words such as those for *grandfather* and *grandmother*, *milk*, *boy*, *girl* and *now* which vary between North and South Wales, could profitably be introduced in the early stages of learning, grammatical differences could easily confuse beginning learners. Most native speakers are, however, aware of the differences and with a little effort could accommodate learners.

Conclusion

The world outside the classroom can be a frightening, confusing place for the learner and, even in homes where there are ready-made opportunities to practise, learners often encounter problems. If learners do not receive a positive response when they first use the language, they may lose confidence and withdraw, believing their Welsh to be inadequate. Learners are not usually prepared for the gulf between learning in class and using/practising Welsh in the community. They also face a range of obstacles in relation to authentic language use in everyday life as opposed to the idealised language of the classroom – the speed of speech, their limited understanding that code switching and code mixing are normal features of interaction in stable bilingual communities and their unfamiliarity with regional variation.

Formal classes can provide help by preparing learners for what they should expect. But native speakers also need to be encouraged to adapt their speech when talking to learners, particularly in the early stages. Learners, for their part, need help to appreciate the insecurities of many native speakers and the extra patience required to sustain conversation with learners.

Chapter 4
Issues of Culture and Identity

> *Language is much more than a means of communication. Not only does it*
> *carry a view of the environment (. . .) but through its vocabulary and its*
> *structure, through the associations generated by its literature, through*
> *the symbol which it is and the symbols which it transmits, it creates a*
> *distinctive identity which is at once a derivative of tradition and an*
> *expression of the present.*
> Aitchison & Carter, 1994: 6

Issues of language, culture and identity are inextricably entwined for any learner who wants to continue past the 'get by in . . .' stage. Languages are vehicles of culture and open doors to unknown worlds where hidden treasures intrigue, inspire and sometimes disquiet the learner. This chapter looks at a range of further issues that may affect learners' willingness to continue to learn and use an L2. It focuses, in particular, on adult learners' construction of their identity as Welsh-speakers.

More Than Just Language

The transition from classroom to community is a struggle for most learners that involves both linguistic and non-linguistic dimensions. Learning a language is different from learning most other subjects; as Gardner (2001: 3) points out, 'language is an integral part of the individual and a significant part of the self'. There are countless examples in the (auto) biographical literature of Welsh learners of this awareness. For instance, P. Thomas (2001: 18) observes:

> A language is, after all, far more than just a means of communicating with someone else. Every language has its own unique idioms and resonance. It enshrines a particular and special way of looking at the world.

Alice Traille James (Unidentified, 2002), Learner of the Year 2002, comments in a similar vein:

> Your whole world is enriched when you speak another language and it is important for people moving into Welsh-speaking areas to learn Welsh so that they understand the place they have come to live and the people who live there. It is not just a language that you learn and understand but an ancient culture that is full of things like the *eisteddfodau* and *cynghanedd* [Welsh poetry in strict metre]. It is so much more than just a language and it has helped me to set down new roots here.

Cultural and identity issues were also important to learners interviewed by the WCC (R. Jones, 2005). In almost every group, there was a learner who wanted to regain a language which the previous generation had failed to transmit, not only so that they could speak Welsh, but also to appreciate Wales' culture and literature. One learner commented:

> Basically it's because I'm living in Wales now. I know it sounds trite, but I think there is a failure of myself and many to appreciate that I have really moved into, when I say another country, a place where there is a separate identity and a separate culture and I want to try to gel with that because we live in the area.

What Is Welshness?

Many people do not realise that Wales, like England, is a constituent country of the United Kingdom and not a part of England. The issue of 'Welshness' is a keenly debated topic, particularly in relation to language, as some maintain one has to be Welsh-speaking in order to be Welsh (Betts, 2001). When exploring the idea of Welshness on her world tour in search of Welsh-speakers and learners, Petro (1997: 189–191) encountered the notion of Welshness by degrees:

> If I've heard the phrase, Oh, he or she – usually he – 'is very Welsh' once on this trip I've heard it a thousand times. There seems to be a consensus among the Singaporeans that Eleri is just a little 'more Welsh' than everyone else on the island. I can't imagine a more foreign notion. I would never think to call myself more or less American than anyone else I know. The state of being 'very American' is usually reserved for inanimate objects, like big cars and cheeseburgers (. . .) America, of course, is too plural to pin down to a specific national identity, and too powerful to worry much about it; Wales, on the other hand, is not only tiny but ever-defining itself so it won't wake up one day as England. Nonetheless,

I have a suspicion that language lies at the root of the problem. And this is a problem. (...) Living with a linguistic sliding scale for the past century or more has created what I can only call an atmosphere, or a mindset, of comparison in Wales.

The notion of Welshness by degrees is also noted by writers such as Trosset (1993), Gwyneth Lewis (1998) and D.H. Lewis (2001). It may well be that this phenomenon is more likely to occur within a lesser-used language community, where people react variably to the influence of the majority language.

Although there is no clear definition of Welshness, the experiences and perceptions of adult Welsh learners throw some light upon this issue. Many of the accounts collected by Davies and Bowie (1992), for instance, indicate that a knowledge of Welsh produces a new sense of Welsh identity and a deeper understanding of the people and country, and its traditions and history. In the face of globalisation, lesser-used language communities can provide security for the many learners who embark on an inward search to find a new identity and a sense of belonging. Prys Jones (1992: 11) speaks for many adult learners when describing Welsh language and culture as: 'a bulwark against the flood of the monolithic, vapid Anglo-American culture which has swept through our country in recent decades'. Similarly, Jan Harris (2001) reports that she felt part of the community in Lampeter in South West Wales in a way she never had in the urban areas of London and South East England. Significantly, she believes that she and her family would have lost out if they had not been able to take part in many of the activities in their new home territory because they could not speak the language. Petro (1997: 78) makes a similar point: 'Wales is still rural. I think it's a draw to the pastoral, to the sense of community that you don't get in a city (. . .) The language gives you entry to a world that's disappearing everywhere else'.

These are not, of course, isolated cases: many Welsh learners at home and abroad are motivated by the quest for *Gemeinschaft* [community] within *Gesellschaft* [society] (Khleif, 1978). Whereas post modern commentators reject historical continuity – whether ethnic, cultural or linguistic – many people claim to have found a new satisfying identity within the framework of a restored or adopted language and culture (May, 2000: 38–9). However, it is only in the more rural communities in North West and West Wales that the sense of community appreciated by Petro and Harris is still apparent today. It is possible to argue that the community spirit that existed even in fairly large towns before World War II in Wales, as described by Rosser (1989), has disappeared, never to return.

Identity is very closely linked to a sense of belonging. As Lewis (2001: 1) comments in relation to participants on an intensive Welsh course: 'They wished to belong. They wished to participate fully in Welshness on an equal footing with the native Welsh-speaker'. N. Jones (1993: 20) comments in a similar vein: 'Learning Welsh as a second language – for a person from Wales – means sorting out identity. It cleans up ambiguity about belongingness and it means defining relations'. Bowie (1993: 171) suggests that many Welsh learners believe they can be widely accepted in the community and make a valid contribution particularly if, through marriage or other kinship links, they can be placed within the tight-knit web of relations, which characterise Welsh-speaking Wales. She observes that some learners adopt a new identity and 'go native', exclusively mixing with Welsh-speakers and endeavouring to find work through the medium of Welsh. Some even change their names, play down any non-Welsh links, and join the more radical Welsh language movements (Bianchi, 1992). Such learners go beyond integration, seeking rather assimilation and the desire to be indistinguishable from native speakers, something very hard to achieve however competent the learner and however close the accent and intonation of the learner is to that of mother tongue speakers (Morgan, 2000).

Other learners, however, may be uncomfortable with the Welsh interest in origins and may experience feelings of anomie or uncertainty about one's place and one's loyalties within the new language group (Burdett-Jones, 2004; Newcombe, 2004). Learners are attracted by the new but experience conflict because of emotional ties to the old, and can become anxious that too deep an involvement with L2 culture will result in alienation from their own community. Students may fear loss of ethnic identity and uncertainty about their place in both cultures. Trosset (1984: 42) comments that such uncertainty can characterise not only the socially unattached but also the bilingual or even the serious student of a second language and culture. Second language learners may never attain native-like proficiency because they may find that the reward of being fluent in the target language cannot compensate for the lost identification and solidarity with their own native language group. Feelings of anomie may hinder the progress of some learners on the path to fluency; the practicalities of keeping pace with two social orbits may intensify feelings of conflict. This situation is further complicated in Wales if only one member of a family chooses to learn Welsh and be integrated into Welsh society, particularly in an area such as Cardiff where Welsh is not the language of the community. Learners, however, can select the aspects of Welsh identity they wish to adopt. As Wray *et al.* (2003: 69) have argued:

Through tourism, the broadcast media and the internet we have the opportunity to dip into a much wider range of cultural influence. It is possible to adopt aspects of a Welsh social identity without displacing some other identity.

The notion of multiple identities, from which individuals can choose both according to situation and at different points in their lives, characterises most recent discussions of identity. Thus Hampâté Ba (1996), a West African diplomat, identifies at least three separate identities for himself: the adult operating in Fulani society, the administrator and diplomat – the product of colonialism, and the man educated in French culture. It is common to acquire parallel identities for people living in multilingual, multicultural societies, as suggested by the hyphenation in discussions of Cuban-Americans, Gaelic-Canadians, Chinese-Malay and German-Australians. Baker and Prys Jones (1998: 25), for instance, argue that in communities of this kind, 'confusion of identity is replaced by a unique integration of values and beliefs, allowing a person to bridge two language groups and mingle on either side'.

Dual and/or multiple identities are issues for serious consideration in sustaining the motivation of L2 learners, whether one is learning Welsh in Wales, English in Canada or German in Germany. Some learners have no difficulty in assuming a new identity (see, for instance, Stavans, 2002) but others flounder and some (for instance, Rodriguez, 1981) even reject their original ethnic identity in favour of their adopted identity. As indicated earlier, such instances occur in the Welsh context (Bianchi, 1992). These are issues that cannot be divorced from learning and using an L2 and need to be addressed by L2 educators and researchers.

A Welsh Identity

The situation of adult learners in Wales is, of course, very different from that of language minority speakers learning the majority language. Nonetheless, language plays a range of roles in the ways learners construct their Welsh identity. O. Davies (1992: 75) believes he became 'really Welsh' when he mastered the language:

> How could we ever claim to be one of 'them' when what made them 'really Welsh' was precisely that language, which we did not know? Welsh – those familiar but incomprehensible words – seemed an unbridgeable barrier between what they were and what we were: their fate and ours (...) I seemed to be becoming 'really Welsh' in that more precious way.

Gillibrand (1992), now a fluent Welsh-speaker and tutor, holds that he has a dual national identity, Welsh and English, and that he is considered to be a Welshman by his English siblings. Barnie (1992: 121), in contrast, maintains that learning Welsh as an adult is not sufficient to make one 'really' Welsh. Originally from an anglicised area in South Wales, but now living in a Welsh heartland area, he believes that he will never 'become' Welsh: 'Thirteen years in Denmark taught me that, for most, the language you are brought up in is the water in which you must swim'. Prys Jones (1992) believes that, although she will never quite be 'really Welsh', her children will be, because they have received a Welsh-medium education in a Welsh heartland area.

Questions of identity are particularly complicated in Wales, where learners include English and other incomers as well as Welsh people from Anglicised areas where the language has been lost for several generations. The present inhabitants of South East Wales, for instance, cannot be held responsible for the gradual disappearance of the language and culture of their forebears. Many of these are people who only know a few words of Welsh but stake a resolute claim to Welshness. As Duggan (1992: 140) comments:

> It is unjust to stigmatise their inhabitants as half-breeds and turncoats, and still less as traitors, because they have lost, through no fault of their own, the language of their grandparents and all that went with it. Everything else about them proclaims, very loudly indeed, that they, too, are of the *Cymry* [Welsh-speaking Welsh people], and in the tale of the sorrows of Wales their lament is as great as any.

Moreover, these are people who feel Welsh. This is why it is not surprising that in South East Wales there has been such a boom in adults learning Welsh. As Cennard Davies (1980: 42–3) observes:

> For the majority of non-Welsh-speaking valley residents, the language is not a remote phenomenon anyway, but a matter of relatively recent family history, with Welsh-speakers only two or three generations removed or even contemporaries in another branch of the extended family.

These people, then, have what could be termed in Welsh *anian* [ethos or temperament]. If their Welshness is linguistically limited, it knows no emotional boundaries, and, when the emotions are stirred and people feel a sense of loss, they are arguably more likely to persevere in restoring their family language than those who do so for more pragmatic reasons. Many successful learners have indicated that, though they *felt* Welsh before they knew the language of their homeland and ancestors, they were not content until they could converse in the language. Aran Jones, for instance, one of the finalists in the Learner of the Year competition in 2003, wrote that before he could speak Welsh 'there was a part of me missing'. After Aran's story was posted on the web, other learners wrote identifying with his sentiments (A. Jones, 2003).

Discussion of identity among Welsh people who no longer speak the language is extensive. Smith (1984: 152) records the reminiscences of the writer, Gwyn Thomas, whose parents did not transmit the Welsh language:

> My father and mother were Welsh-speaking yet I did not exchange a word in that language with them. The death of Welsh ran through our family like a geological fault. Places like the Rhondda were parts of America that never managed to get the boat.

At university in a Welsh heartland area in the 1970s, Vivienne Sayer was surprised to encounter denial of her Welshness by speakers, who regarded her as 'a second class citizen, third class really, because at least the English had an excuse'. She was aware of condemnation because she could not speak the language but was not encouraged to learn it and formed the distinct impression that learners were held in fairly low esteem (Sayer, 1998).

The situation of 'the Welsh identified learner' is arguably even more complex in the Welsh heartlands. Roger, a participant in the AWLP, learned some Welsh informally as a student in Aberystwyth in the late 1960s and early 1970s but observed a rift between Welsh-speakers and other Welsh people. The Welsh-speakers he encountered 'did not seem to accept that there was a place for learners', 'they kept in their own exclusive group'.

Bowie (1993) describes the distress of learners who have grown up in South Wales and moved to Gwynedd in the North West when they realised they were regarded as 'English'. She believes that Welsh and English can be used as ciphers for 'insider' and 'outsider', and serve to distance incomers from locals and learners from first-language Welsh-speakers. However, this is to misunderstand the meaning of the words *Saeson/Saesnes* [literally, English man/English woman] in North Wales. The terms are used by Welsh-speakers to describe English-speakers and does not necessarily imply that they are not part of Welsh society (Hughes, 2006). R. Roberts (2002) makes a similar point. He was brought up in Swansea, a non-heartland area. His family had lost its Welsh language two generations earlier. Ironically, however, his 'Welshness' extended far further back than that of some of the Welsh-speakers who mocked his early efforts to learn Welsh. Roberts concludes that some Welsh-speakers are obsessed with family roots. They wish to keep the language for their own clique and are unwelcoming to learners, chuckling behind their backs at their efforts to learn the language. An ambivalent attitude to minority language learners by native speakers is not unique to the Welsh-speaking areas of Wales but also attested to in other cultures. N. Jones (1993: 40) cites French Catalonia as an example of such ambivalence.

Attitudes towards Welsh learners have, however, undergone a significant change in recent years. Trosset's (1993) ethnographic study of the linguistic situation into which learners must move indicates that, whilst a small minority of L1 speakers resent the intrusion of learners into the Welsh language community, the majority express approval of learners' dedication and progress. K. Jones (2000: 648) describes similar findings in a study of in-migrants[1] to North East Wales. Although the in-migrants reported feeling that some Welsh-speakers associated Welsh with an 'in-group' code and were therefore reluctant to use it with non-Welsh outsiders, most Welsh-speakers were willing to accept learners' efforts to use Welsh. Similarly, Philip, a participant in the AWLP, observed that, although hindered by the clannishness of the Welsh-speakers in college about 40 years ago, most native speakers are now more willing to support his efforts; this was also the general view of others involved in this study. Supportive attitudes, however, do not necessarily extend to children. Andrea recorded that she had recently overheard children from Welsh-speaking homes make patronising comments to children from English-only homes attending Welsh-medium school.

Sometimes, however, observations made by native speakers are perceived by learners as patronising. As Bohren (1978) observed when opening the Learners' Tent in the 1978 National Eisteddfod, the word *dysgwr* [learner] carries nuances of inferiority. Bohren favours the word *mabwysiadwyr* [adopters] as learners do not wish to be categorised as learners when they are able to use the language in the community. Cook (2002) argues that the motivation for using the term L2 user 'is the feeling that it is demeaning to call someone who has functioned in an L2 environment for years a *learner* rather than a *user*'. However, the word *dysgwr* continues to be used in Wales for learners at all levels and native speakers may, albeit unintentionally, upset learners when they attach the label. Sioned, for instance, reported feeling daunted on hearing Welsh-speakers saying, 'They are good but I could tell they were learners'. Gareth Kiff, a senior tutor at Cardiff University, advises the learner not to overreact to comments of this kind which, he believes, are often intended as a compliment. Sometimes, native speakers are amazed at the high standard of a learner's fluency and accuracy in Welsh (Roberts & Davies, 2002). Becoming fluent in an L2 in the United Kingdom is often seen as a special achievement rather than the norm, even though it is common in many parts of the world for individuals to speak more than one language (Baker, 2001). As Gardner (2001: 1) comments: 'Some cultures accept learning more than one language as a simple fact of life; others consider it a relatively rare and difficult event'.

Conclusion

The issues discussed in Chapter 3 – the tendency for native speakers to switch to English, the speed of speech, dialect and code switching – were all recognised by learners as potential barriers to progress as they made the transition from classroom to community. In contrast, the issues of language, culture and identity explored in the present chapter provoked a wide variety of responses from L2 learners. Because identity is closely linked with notions of inclusion and exclusion, this is an area of considerable importance for learner success.

We all embrace a range of different and sometimes conflicting loyalties: as the discussion in this chapter has demonstrated, there is no single Welsh identity or set of cultural norms. Identity varies both across time and from one individual to the next. Traditional Welsh culture, for instance, was linked with Welsh religious non-conformity, and chapel life was the centre of the social life of a Welsh-speaking community. *Eisteddfodau* were central to the cultural lives of most Welsh-speakers. Currently, a variety of new domains, for instance pop music bands and dance, are associated with Welshness and Welsh is increasingly permeating the world of business and commerce. Thus, if learners feel excluded from one domain they are able to move to another where they feel more accepted.

It is vital that learners are prepared to face issues of this kind in the early stages of learning so that they are not shocked and dismayed if they encounter native speakers who – deliberately or inadvertently – create the impression that learners have no place in Welsh-speaking communities. It is also vital that learners do not become linguistically marginalised and remain in their own group, for as Trosset (1986) warns, the language development of those who do not use their L2 skills with native speakers will inevitably fossilise.

Bowie (1993) is probably right in seeing the Welsh learner as the 'joker in the pack' who does not fit neatly into either 'English' or 'Welsh'. She also notes, however, that the learner 'can play both cards'. Fluent Welsh learners, in particular, have the potential to play a crucial bridging role between Welsh learners and Welsh-speakers as they have an understanding of both groups and may act as role models. This is certainly true in the areas of culture and identity but, as indicated in Chapter 3, it is possible for some learners who have progressed to L2 speaker to forget the linguistic needs of learners and the value of sustaining conversations with them in the target language.

Notes

1. It appears that the term 'in-migrant' has come to be used in the Welsh context, rather than the more established term 'immigrant', to avoid the implicit connotation of foreignness. 'Immigrant' suggests someone who comes from another

country, whereas 'in-migrant' is quite likely to be someone from the same country/state but who has previously lived in another area within that country/state. Most 'in-migrants' in Wales are from other parts of the United Kingdom. It is also sometimes assumed that an immigrant is part of a disadvantaged community within the host state, perhaps open to discrimination, perhaps without legal rights, disadvantaged financially and in terms of material resources. Within the context of in-migration in Wales, it can be argued that the host community is disadvantaged in terms of its relations to the in-migrating population; in terms of financial and material resources (which are less than those of the in-migrating population as a whole), and also in terms of linguistic and cultural matters (as the in-migrating population carries the official, privileged language of the State and its accompanying culture).

Chapter 5
Anxiety and Lack of Confidence

Language anxiety ranks high among factors influencing language learning,
regardless of whether the setting is informal (language learning 'on the streets') or formal
(in the language classroom)
Oxford, 1999: 59

Introduction

Until the latter half of the 20th century, affective variables such as attitude, motivation and anxiety were rarely accorded importance in accounts of differences in the progress of second language learners. Today, however, there is a greater awareness that such variables play a crucial role. This chapter looks at how anxiety and lack of confidence impact on L2 learners' progress and willingness to practise. It considers the importance learners attach to these issues, and the extent to which anxiety is a trait associated with the learning situation or the individual learner.

Affective Factors in Language Learning

There is evidence that anxious language learners tend to underestimate and relaxed students to overestimate their level of proficiency (MacIntyre *et al.*, 1997). As MacIntyre (2002: 67) suggests: 'If this represents a prevalent tendency, then anxious language learners will tend to remain anxious because they tend to withdraw from situations that might increase their proficiency, creating a self-fulfilling prophecy'. If MacIntyre and Gardner (1989) are right that students experience anxiety only after repeated negative experiences, it is therefore of vital importance that all unnecessary stress and friction are eliminated.

The place of anxiety as a barrier to language learning is currently viewed as one of the main factors impeding effective L2 learning (Gardner, 2001). Anxiety is also believed to affect the extent to which learners are prepared to apply their learning. MacIntyre (1995: 96), for instance, observes that:

> If anxiety arises during learning then anxious students will perform poorly because they have learned less. However, if anything anxiety may be more strongly aroused by speaking than by learning. Thus anxiety may also interfere with the student's ability to demonstrate the amount that she or he knows.

Horwitz' (2001) review of the literature on foreign language anxiety endorses this view and concludes that anxiety has been almost entirely associated with the oral aspects of language use. Indeed, the studies included confirm the widely held intuitive views of tutors that anxiety inhibits language learning and use. A recent study on EFL in China has demonstrated that students felt less anxious as they became more proficient and the more they were exposed to the target language; however, they were particularly anxious when singled out in class but less anxious when participating in pair work (Liu, 2006).

Earl Stevick (1976, 1996) coined the phrase 'lathophobic aphasia' to describe learners' unwillingness to speak another language for fear of making mistakes; avoidance of foreign language situations, addiction to continuous classroom training, and the feeling that native L2 speakers would not welcome the learner's use of their native tongue are regarded as manifestations of the phenomenon. Most of the students in the AWLP exhibited such lathophobic aphasia to a greater or lesser degree for, as Horwitz (2001: 118) has indicated, 'Anxious language learners feel uncomfortable with their abilities even if their objective abilities are good'. Alan and Philip have particularly good oral skills in Welsh but on several occasions disclosed that they had missed good opportunities to practise the language with native speakers because of their fears. Similarly, Rees, who has a particularly wide vocabulary and an excellent understanding of grammar, admitted at focus group that he often avoided speaking to native speakers in Welsh because of his general diffidence. Likewise, Sharon, not quite such an experienced learner, but nevertheless able to hold a conversation wrote:

> At Mother & Toddler today it was busy and I managed to speak Welsh to a few people. I am using it more with the children but the more I do the journal the more I realise how little I am making the most of the opportunities to use my Welsh. But it is very hard to summon up the confidence, which is definitely the biggest problem!

Kim, in contrast, while admitting some lost opportunities, did not see anxiety as a major problem: 'If I make a mistake people have to accept that I am trying'.

Agnes was particularly anxious and this is probably why, like Rees, her journal entries described her reading and writing rather than speaking experiences. She indicated when interviewed that she was afraid of what native speakers would say in response to her speaking efforts and, in a focus group discussion, volunteered: 'I cannot cope with talking to people on the street'. Interestingly, Alice, the beginner, exhibited little anxiety. She indicated in the focus group that lack of confidence was low on her list of problems despite her limited knowledge and she was willing to practise with native speakers at any opportunity. She attributed her attitude to years of living in France when she 'had to do everything through French'.

Since the 1970s, an influential and sometimes controversial view of the relationship between acquisition and learning an L2 propounded by Stephen Krashen (1977) has become popular and widely disseminated. The emphasis on acquisition leads Krashen to propose an 'input hypothesis' which suggests that tutors should try to reproduce in the classroom the conditions that occur in L1 acquisition. For the purposes of this discussion, Krashen's affective filter hypothesis (Dulay *et al.*, 1982) is of particular interest: the hypothesis describes the need for second-language learning to occur in an environment of low anxiety, to encourage the processing and learning of new information. The filter encompasses affective factors such as attitudes to language, motivation, self-confidence and anxiety. Learners with favourable attitudes and self-confidence may have 'a low filter' and may therefore be more receptive to L2 input. Those with 'high filters' have high anxiety levels and/or unfavourable attitudes and may be less receptive to L2 input. As this chapter unfolds, it will become clear that many of the learners discussed have 'high affective filters' and will need to find ways forward before crossing the bridge from being L2 learners to L2 speakers.

Some of the learners in the present study were clearly willing to take such risks. Sioned, for instance, contrasted herself with her sister, an academic who is good at languages but who, until recently, has been unwilling to speak the language in real life situations despite her qualifications in Welsh. Although less advanced than her sister, she is ready to 'give it a go'. Similarly, Roger compared his wife's attitude to languages to his own. In France, he is always the one to converse with native speakers even though his wife knows a great deal more French; he, too, is always willing to 'have a go'. Rees, despite an extended vocabulary and a good foundation in grammar, was far more reluctant to speak Welsh than his wife whose knowledge was minimal. Sioned, Roger's wife and Rees' wife are clearly willing to take risks in order to communicate in Welsh, despite limited competence in the language.

Many language learners, however, find risk taking difficult and, in extreme cases, their anxiety results in unwillingness to communicate at all. Various writers draw attention to this phenomenon. Smith (1987), for instance, reports the comment of a second language learner about a class they had once attended: 'I began to dread going – when he picked on me I nearly died'. Tsui (1996) similarly observes that fear of being derided for mistakes by tutors or other students can make students reticent in class.

Although tutors may think they are saving students embarrassment by stepping in, their intervention often has the effect of increasing anxiety; many learners merely need more time to formulate their answer or to have the question paraphrased. As a practitioner, I have experienced this pattern of events on several occasions and in a variety of groups. Students have shouted out either to me or other students: 'Don't tell me. Wait!' indicating that they think they know the appropriate response but need more time for recall.

If students dislike premature intervention in the classroom, they are likely to be even more anxious when it happens in a naturalistic setting such as the home, the community or workplace. In focus group discussions, students indicated that the classroom was a much more secure setting than the real world. Outside the classroom, they often feel demoralised when Welsh-speakers, out of kindness or impatience, and, on occasions, somewhat patronizingly, provide the correct Welsh word or phrase or switch to English instead of allowing them time to work out the appropriate response.

Adults tend to be more reluctant to take risks than children: they often doubt their ability to learn and fear looking silly or being rejected if they make mistakes. Schumann (1986: 382) refers to this phenomenon as 'language shock' and cites work by Stengal (1939) who believed that adults often fear they will appear comic. Stengal compares learning a second language by adults to a person wearing fancy clothes. The adult learner may want to wear his fancy clothes but is inhibited by fear of ridicule and criticism. The child, on the other hand, sees language as a form of play and enjoys wearing his fancy clothes. The more of 'these infantile characteristics' adults have preserved, the more easily they will learn the L2 (Stengal, 1939: 475–6). C.S. Lewis (Hooper, 1966: 25) similarly held that the most adult among us are those who have lost the fear of seeming childish: 'When I became a man I put away childish things, including the fear of childishness and the desire to be very grown up'. It is certainly my experience as a tutor that the students who are willing to take risks and experiment with language to the extent of making themselves look foolish are often the more successful language learners in the long term.

Learner Perceptions of Confidence

Lack of confidence would appear to be a common phenomenon in second language learners. It was discussed at length in focus groups for the present study. Evidence from a questionnaire completed by participants after the focus groups also suggests that anxiety is a major obstacle to successful learning. Students were asked to record on a 5 point Likert scale their reactions to several statements including: 'I am confident when I practise speaking or listening to Welsh' (see Table 5.1).

Table 5.1 Response to statement: 'I am confident when I practise speaking or listening to Welsh'

Agree strongly	Agree	Neutral	Disagree	Disagree strongly
0	2	3	8	1

Nine disagreed, one disagreed strongly, three were neutral and only two agreed with the statement; no one agreed strongly. This response was perhaps particularly surprising in the light of the fact that only one of the students was a complete beginner when the study began.

Lack of confidence also had a high profile in a card sorting exercise where students were asked to place 13 items reported as difficulties in learner journals in order of importance. 13 of the 14 learners taking part in this exercise returned their cards as a single deck arranged in order. The other respondent returned her cards in two packs: 6 items that were important to her arranged in order, and 7 unimportant ones, separately. The 14 respondents' rankings for the 13 items are shown in Table 5.2 and discussion of the analysis appears in Figure 5.1.

Of particular significance for the present discussion is the importance attached to lack of confidence, the level of agreement between respondents being substantial. It is possible to argue, of course, that this item ranks highly because it was the only problem internal to the learner. However, it also figured prominently in the journals of all but two of the learners. Interestingly, some of the students who presented as confident when interviewed challenged this perception in their journal entries. Roger, for instance, saw himself as 'lacking confidence' when using Welsh outside class despite the fact that, in the classroom, he contributed more than any

Table 5.2 Rankings of 13 difficulties by 14 respondents, and overall consensus ranks

	Kim	Rees	Alan	Agnes	Cathy	Andrea	Alice	Sharon
Lack of confidence	6	2	5	3	3	7	5	1
Life through medium of English	11	1	4	2	1	1	1	4
Welsh-speakers, too quickly	5	4	2	4	4	5	10	2
Lack time to practise or study	8	12	8	1	7	2	2	3
Welsh-speakers turning to English	1	5	3	9	5	6	3	5
Difference class vs. real world	2	3	7	6	2	8	6	7
Welsh-speakers use slang	4	7	6	7	10	10	4	9
Welsh-speakers, too much dialect	3	6	10	5	9	9	11	10
Will never be accepted by L1 speakers	10	9	1	11	8	13	9	8
Insufficient support, non-Welsh family	12	10	9	12	12	4	8	11
Insufficient support L1 family and friends	7	11	12	13	6	12	7	13
Non-Welsh-speakers surprised/opposed	13	13	13	10	13	3	13	6
Welsh-speakers surprise/disdain	9	8	11	8	11	11	12	12

(*Continued*)

Table 5.2 Continued

	Sioned	Philip	Clare	Laura	Lydia	Roger	Overall ranks	
							Unweighted	Top down
Lack of confidence	2	2	3	1	1	3	1	2
Life through medium of English	5	9	2	6	2	1	2	1
Welsh-speakers, too quickly	1	1	4	3	5	8	3	3
Lack time to practise or study	4	6	1	8	3	2	4	4
Welsh-speakers turning to English	6	5	10	4	4	6	5	5
Difference class vs. real world	7	13	5	5	8	4	6	6
Welsh-speakers use slang	8	3	10	2	7	10	7	7
Welsh-speakers, too much dialect	9	4	6	7	6	11	8	8
Will never be accepted by L1 speakers	3	11	10	9	9	7	9	9
Insufficient support, non-Welsh family	10	7	10	13	12	9	10	10
Insufficient support L1 family and friends	11	12	10	10	13	5	11	11
Non-Welsh-speakers surprised/opposed	12	8	10	11	10	13	12	12
Welsh-speakers surprise/disdain	13	10	10	12	11	12	13	13

Analysis of card sort results:

13 items that were reported as difficulties in the journals were printed on cards and distributed to 14 respondents, 5 at the start of each of the 2 focus groups and 4 who were unable to take part in these groups. Respondents were asked to sort the 13 cards in order of importance. 13 responders returned their cards as a single deck arranged in order. The other respondent (Clare) commented that it would not be meaningful to order 7 of the items, which were no problem to her. She returned her cards in two packs, 6 items that were important to her arranged in order, and 7 unimportant ones separately. The 14 respondents' rankings for the 13 items are shown in Table 5.2.

In accordance with convention, the tied ranks for Clare's unimportant items were replaced by their average value, 10. The results were entered into SPSS, and the Kendall coefficient of concordance calculated as 0.509, indicating a substantial degree of agreement between the 14 respondents' views of the importance of the 13 items, which was highly statistically significant ($\chi^2 = 85.6$, d.f. = 12, $p < 0.001$). The rank ordering of the average of these unweighted ranks for the 13 items is shown in the penultimate column of the table. The 13 items are presented in the order of these unweighted rank averages.

Clare's perceptive comment suggested that the above conventional analysis, which regards differences between ranks 1 and 2 and between ranks 12 and 13 as equally important, may not be optimal. An alternative analysis that downweights differences at the lower end of the scale is described by Zar (1999). This analysis leads to a top–down concordance $C_T = 0.434$, still highly significant ($\chi^2 = 72.9$, d.f. = 12, $p < 0.001$). The final column of the table gives the corresponding consensus rankings.

The two approaches to the analysis lead to quite similar conclusions. Both analyses show a degree of agreement between respondents that is not perfect but is very substantial. The two most important items are lack of confidence and life through the medium of English. These come close to each other in importance and which one comes out on top depends on whether the unweighted or weighted analysis is chosen. The positions of the remaining 11 items are identical on both approaches.

Lack of confidence might be expected to be ranked high merely because it is the only item on the list that is internal to the learner. However, it figured in all but 2 of the journals and 1 of the journal writers who did not write about it expressed strong feelings on her lack of confidence when speaking at interview and in the focus group. One of the learners, Alice who did not mention the issue was hardly using the language for speaking as her only Welsh-speaking contact had left the area. She attributes her confident attitude when using Welsh to the fact that she lived for some years in France and 'had to do everything through French'. The other student, Agnes, was using Welsh mainly for reading and listening to the media. However, this student, at interview and at a focus group, made it clear that she was lacking in confidence when speaking and expressed a strong preference for reading. This indicates that lack of confidence is not placed high on the list of rankings solely because it is the only item of its kind. Moreover, it became increasingly clear at focus groups that lack of confidence, as well as being important in its own right, also coloured the reaction of learners to many other barriers mentioned, in particular:

- Welsh-speakers switching to English
- Welsh-speakers' speed of speech
- Welsh-speakers using dialect
- Welsh-speakers using a low-level language register/Welsh/English combinations
- Difference between classroom and the real world
- Welsh-speakers not accepting learners 'as part of the club'.

Figure 5.1 Analysis of card sort results

other student in the group. Although Andrea reported that she used every possible opportunity to speak Welsh, both with those she knew well and those she met casually, she also felt daunted by what she perceived to be Welsh-speakers' pedantic corrections.

In focus group discussions, lack of confidence not only emerged as important in its own right, but also coloured the reaction of learners to many other barriers, including the tendency for Welsh-speakers to switch to English; the speed of Welsh-speakers' speech; Welsh-speakers' use of dialect; differences between classroom and the real world; and the reluctance of Welsh-speakers to accept learners 'as part of the club'. Lack of confidence and anxiety are evident in both learners' perceptions of their efforts at conversation and in the reactions of others to these efforts. It seems probable that objective problems are accentuated in learners' minds by fear.

It is possible, of course, that social forces were leading students to exaggerate the importance of confidence issues. It is certainly a feature of Welsh culture, particularly in past generations, not 'to show off' or 'put yourself forward'. Perryman (2004), in an entirely different context, always felt she had to downplay her progress in the Chinese language because of similar Chinese expectations. The importance many learners attributed to low levels of confidence, however, would suggest that this interpretation is unlikely.

Tutors also drew attention to confidence issues. As Gwen Awbery, co-ordinating lecturer for Welsh at LEARN, Cardiff University, pointed out: 'It is a very public act to use an L2. Learners can feel crushed and patronised if they are not given appropriate help and can feel "put-down" if native speakers cease to use the target language'. Lack of confidence also affects reactions in relation to the issues raised in Chapters 3 and 4. For instance, Welsh-speakers' speed of speech, elisions and dialect features may cause the anxious learner to panic and switch to English instead of asking in Welsh for the sentence to be repeated. Similarly, identity issues may appear more problematic to the anxious learner. However, this is something of a 'chicken and egg' situation: it is difficult to be sure in individual cases whether anxiety triggers an adverse reaction or whether particular circumstances trigger anxiety.

Trait or state anxiety

Schumann (1986: 382) observes that capable students often derive a good deal of 'narcissistic gratification' from their use of their L1 and use language to gain attention and praise. They lose such gratification, however, when speaking in a second language in which they are far less proficient. Tsui (1996: 156) makes a similar point: 'When communicating in a language in which they are not fluent, learners cannot help but feel that they are not fully representing their personality and their intelligence'. Kinney (1992: 2) provides support for this position as she reflects on her own language learning:

> Anything I had to say would be peppered with mistakes, and I am a lover
> of language. I love the process of choosing the precise word to bring out

a subtle meaning, of turning a phrase in such a way as to shed a new light on a topic. And I knew that as far as the Welsh language was concerned I could not say what I wanted to say but what I was able to say.

Similarly, Lewis (1999), who learned Welsh in New Zealand in the 1980s, commented in her journal:

My biggest lack is still not being able to sustain a normal conversation. Anything I can say is still determined by the words I know rather than by the ideas in my head.

A female in her sixties from Gwynedd, North West Wales, interviewed as part of a research project by the WCC expressed similar sentiments: 'You become a child again, struggling to find the words in Welsh, if you transfer to English that power balance is even again, you aren't so vulnerable. Take away your ability to communicate effectively and you really are like a child' (R. Jones, 2005). Horwitz (2001: 114) attributes such reactions to the complex and non-spontaneous mental operations that are necessary in order to converse at all. Thus, any performance in an L2 may well challenge an individual's self-image as an adept communicator and 'lead to reticence, self-consciousness, fear, or even panic'.

However, anxiety does not always derive from the situation. Since the 1970s, scholars have distinguished between trait and state anxiety in language learning (Scovel, 1978). Trait anxiety refers to an individual's tendency to become anxious in any situation, whereas state anxiety refers to apprehension experienced in certain situations and/or at a particular moment in time, for example, having to speak in an L2 in front of others. More recently, the term situation-specific anxiety has been used to emphasise the persistent and multi-faceted nature of some anxieties such as public speaking anxiety (MacIntyre & Gardner, 1991) and experts are now taking the position that foreign language anxiety falls also into this category (Horwitz, 2001). Some AWLP students exhibited trait anxiety. Laura, for instance, indicated that she lacked confidence and panicked if she has to contribute to any large group discussion, in English as well as in Welsh. Interestingly, she is happy listening to Welsh and copes quite well at work meetings held in Welsh: 'I tend to be able to get the gist of what's going on, even if I don't always get it word for word'. The problem, then, would rather seem to be related to her background level of anxiety. Equally interestingly, when her level of anxiety was decreased by the informality of a residential stay in a language centre in North West Wales, her difficulties were markedly reduced:

Nant Gwrtheryn was an excellent experience. I went in a group of ten people from my workplace for five days. I found that I got on well partly because I was there with friends and didn't feel intimidated or nervous in front of them. I also knew what level they were at and could learn in a fun atmosphere. The fact that we were staying at the Centre helped a lot – we didn't have to worry about the normal day-to-day stuff like work, cooking dinner and shopping so we could devote more time to learning and keep our minds programmed. I have thought about going back again but I really don't think I would get as much out of it if I went on my own (due to lack of confidence mainly). If I was invited to go with a group again, I would jump at the chance! (...) I was even dreaming in Welsh by the time I left!

Some learners, however, rationalise their lack of confidence in other ways. Sharon, Cathy and Rees, for instance, equated limited confidence to some extent with laziness. This was very clear in one of Sharon's journal entries:

Spoke a little with the Welsh-speaking childminder but got chatting and the conversation reverted to English, but I have asked her to be stricter with me over this as I think I need to be nudged back into Welsh when I lose confidence or feel too lazy.

Rees also attributed his lack of practice at every available opportunity to laziness, a quality he believes he shares with other learners: 'We are all lazy'. However, other comments suggest his problem was far deeper. Given his extensive receptive knowledge of the language, his reluctance to speak is more likely a function of his anxiety about making mistakes. Although only records of speaking and listening were requested for journal research, Rees' entries were mainly about reading books and newspapers and were of a standard indicating that, like Laura, he had sufficient knowledge to hold conversations but was not confident to do so. Interestingly, as indicated earlier, Rees volunteered that his wife, who is a learner with a far less developed command of grammar or vocabulary than his, was more confident about speaking Welsh.

Three learners, Mervyn, Anna, and Cliff, interviewed at the National Eisteddfod, also demonstrated how extroversion and introversion may influence progress. Mervyn, an extrovert, reported that he had wanted to learn Welsh because the only ones in his household unable to speak Welsh were himself and the cat. He spoke naturally and, though there were some errors and English insertions, he communicated well in Welsh. Anna, a similarly outgoing person, tried to use the Welsh she has learned at every possible opportunity, despite the fact that she sometimes experienced difficulty in understanding. Cliff, in contrast, was an introvert. Although his grounding in the language was firmer and his access to native speakers easier, his natural shyness meant that he was not availing himself of the opportunities to practice Welsh in the same way as Anna and Mervyn. He attributed his tendency to use the language only when Welsh-speakers initiated the conversation to his lack of confidence.

Extroverts are often stereotyped as being outgoing and talkative and, therefore, better language learners, as they are more likely to contribute in the class and welcome opportunities to practise. Introverts, in contrast, are considered to be less apt language learners as their reserve may hold them back from taking risks. As Arnold and Brown (1999) observe, however, there is not necessarily a causal connection between inhibition and introversion. Extroversion is also related to the need for receiving ego enhancement and a sense of wholeness from other people; introverts, in contrast, may have a great inner strength of character and demonstrate high degrees of empathy: qualities that are particularly useful for language learning. They may also be prepared to spend more time studying and acquiring vocabulary outside class and may therefore be more equipped to use their language skills in the community. Sally, a quiet introverted person who took part in the AWLP, provided support for this position. Although from outside Wales and with no background in the language, she progressed to a high degree of fluency within four years. She was clearly willing to be involved in risk taking and used her Welsh, sometimes with incorrect mutations and constructions, at every opportunity, despite her general diffidence.

Two steps forward, one step back

Students sometimes perceived lack of confidence as an intermittent problem. Thus Cathy wrote:

> I am surprised at how much I can understand of what the teachers have to say at the parents' evening. We have listened to the same Welsh phrases for the past eight years and so the language was not a problem. It made me realise that most of the time one talks in the same well-worn patterns. (. . .) I was suddenly spoken to in Welsh outside church and failed to understand because I wasn't expecting it. I felt a bit stupid. (. . .) Success at last! A telephone conversation with Lucy. As she is a sympathetic teacher she has the knack of being able to draw my meagre Welsh resources out in some coherent manner. This really boosted my confi-

dence again. Why is learning Welsh such an emotional see-saw of success and failure?

This was not an isolated experience. At another point, Cathy wrote: 'With my son's teacher – I forgot a few words of Welsh. I said 'assembly' instead of service. I felt stupid'. However, later in the week she reported: 'The Welsh is coming back. On the phone with a friend two minutes about arrangement for our boys who are performing in St. David's Hall tonight. Fine'.

The journal entries of a number of other learners illustrated the same 'emotional see-saw'. Some of these were close to fluency. Kim, for instance, wrote:

I went to *** and spoke Welsh to the owner and a parent from school. Both these women insist on answering me in English when I speak to them in Welsh. This used to make me feel very inferior and I would give up and speak English. However, I have noticed lately that in situations such as these I am persisting in Welsh and feel more able to take the attitude 'well, shame on them for not supporting a learner'. (. . .) Today I had to go next door with a phone number. I didn't want to go because I did not feel like speaking Welsh. Well, I went and afterwards – no problem. (. . .) They wait when I try to find the right word and if I go into English for a sentence they do not carry on in English. They go back to Welsh.

Not all of Kim's attempts at speaking Welsh, however, were so successful. In a later entry she wrote:

Had a bit of a 'bad day' today speaking Welsh to Brian's teacher, could not seem to find the words, made mistakes – feel like I will never be comfortable in Welsh.

In the focus group discussion, Kim admitted that in the past she had crossed the street rather than encounter a Welsh-speaker and face making conversation. However, by the end of the period during which she kept a journal, she realised that her attitude was changing and perseverance had helped build confidence. She recorded:

I definitely feel I've made a transition now – there are several people in school who now instantly speak Welsh to me, whereas three months ago I rarely spoke Welsh with them and if I did it felt unnatural and didn't last long. (...) Last week I went to have coffee with (. . .) someone who I meet on the road to school and speak Welsh for five minutes so I was quite daunted at the thought of an hour. However, it was very good – I understood the majority of the conversation and the conversation flowed because I fleetingly slipped into English for difficulties but made sure then to return to Welsh. Progress is being made!

In Kim's perception, confidence is linked with native speakers' attitudes to learners. This, of course, is a two-way process: Welsh-speakers are more likely to continue using Welsh with learners who present as confident than with those who appear particularly anxious. By speaking mainly Welsh, but switching to English when there were difficulties, Kim has developed a workable strategy. Philip, an intermittent learner for over 30 years, also shows evidence of strategic thinking about ways to address his limited confidence. In his case, this involved enlisting the support of his wife, Avril, in agreeing a schedule for speaking Welsh to avoid his continuing 'to drift like a rudderless ship':

> On a three day cycle – Day 1 – we have a Welsh conversation when we get up until it is time to get out and do our separate things. Day 2 – we chat if we meet up at lunchtime or, if we don't, at teatime. Day 3 – we share in conversation during the evening. Avril's thinking being that there will be a variety in terms of things pertinent to talk about – one doesn't get into too set a pattern and hopefully it will be quite relaxed.

Scovel (2000) stresses that the anxiety in SLA is an extremely complex area that requires far more research. He emphasises that anxiety in the L2 learner is not always detrimental and may even be enervating, forcing the learner to work harder. Such may have been the case with Kim and Philip. Their anxieties may have prompted a desire to evolve successful strategies.

Confidence and the interlocutor

Learner confidence is sometimes related to the attitudes of the interlocutor. Sharon, Cathy and Sioned reported that their confidence fluctuated according to the attitudes of native speakers and this was the consensus view at focus groups regardless of the degree of anxiety expressed for, as Cathy noted: 'It's all a matter of what you are comfortable with'. Other learners are often perceived as less threatening. There is, of course, a range of problems associated with this course of action: learners are not always aware of their mistakes; their vocabulary is limited; and they tend to switch to English to discuss important matters. While aware of these shortcomings, anxiety and lack of confidence often mean that learners feel more drawn to other learners rather than to native speakers. Sioned wrote:

> It's much easier talking to a Welsh learner especially someone who is roughly on the same level as you because they don't expect too much of you and know how you feel when you are trying to speak Welsh, that is,

having to put in lots of bits of English and expecting to mess things up quite often. You're very willing to help one another out. Sometimes when you're speaking to a fluent Welsh-speaker you feel that they are getting impatient even when they are probably not and I quite often feel that they are expecting me to be better than I am. This is why sometimes if someone asks me something in Welsh I will answer in English because I don't want to let the other person down.

Although some participants in the AWLP reported problems in speaking Welsh to their children (see p. 45), others considered Welsh-speaking children a non-threatening group of interlocutors. Welsh learners often report that they prefer to practise with children rather than adults (Higham, 2002), a phenomenon noted by other L2 learners. Ann Allen (2004), for instance, reported that children with whom she tried to practise Arabic were generally more generous and patient than adults, although an element of ridicule often slipped in. In the present study, Andrea explained that she could keep the conversation simple with children and thereby sustain it. Sharon felt far more comfortable with children and worried that she would impart wrong information to adults. Alan also practises with his own and other children, which he finds easy as so much of the same material is repeated with young children. Laura bemoaned the fact that, in Cardiff, she could not practise with very young children as she had done when living in a heartland area because she had more limited access to Welsh-speakers. In a similar vein, Lydia found reading children's literature a non-threatening learning medium between classes. In spite of its limitations, practising with children is potentially helpful in building learner confidence before they move on to using Welsh with adults.

Conclusion

Widespread learner anxiety is likely to be triggered by and contribute to the various obstacles to progress discussed in earlier chapters. Learner anxiety may well, in turn, be exacerbated by native speakers' anxiety – a problem arguably unique to lesser-used languages, where native speakers' vocabulary and knowledge of various registers is far more variable than that of an L1 speaker of a world language such as English. It is easy in such situations for learners to apportion blame and for the relationships between learners and native speakers to become unnecessarily emotionally charged.

It is possible to argue that, in attempting to use Welsh in the community, the onus is on the learner to be proactive. They need, for instance, to make their wishes clear to native speakers who sometimes are not aware that they wish to practise It is also important to avoid making unreasonable demands on native speakers who cannot always give the time required and may feel insecure about their own competence in Welsh. As Firth and Wagner (1998) point out, language learning does not have a clear end and the distinction between native speakers and advanced second language speakers is not always apparent. Awareness raising of issues of this kind in both L2 class-rooms and among native speakers could help alleviate many of the tensions between learners and native speakers.

Chapter 6
Time and Opportunity

There is no coincidence or simply 'luck' in our life. Everything that happens is the fruit of our work.
Lvovich, 1997: 66

Introduction

Writers such as Benson and Nunan (2004) argue that the processes and goals of language learning are intimately interconnected with other aspects of individuals' lives. Too frequently, students with high motivation cease learning and using an L2 because of life events and/or the pressures of time. The pace of modern life means that there are few who have opportunities for casual conversation. In an account of his attempts to learn English in the United States, for instance, Liu (1984) records how, until he made friends with a young couple, his practice opportunities were very limited. While English permeates life in English-speaking countries, the same is not true of Welsh and other minority languages. Having previously looked at attitudinal barriers to practising Welsh in the community, this chapter focuses on the more practical issues of time and opportunity.

Time

Time is a serious issue for language learners. Two inter-related aspects need to be considered. The first concerns the expectations of students as to how long it will take to achieve fluency in the language. The second concerns how much time is available for study.

The long road to fluency

Some of the AWLP participants were effective and successful language learners. Alan and Sally, for instance, had progressed to Advanced Level standard within three to four years. The experience of many others was very different. Although Brian Church's book, *Learn Greek in 25 Years – for the linguistically challenged*, is not a volume that would ever be placed on a serious language learner's list – and indeed this entertaining book was probably written 'tongue in cheek' – the title nevertheless strikes a chord (Church, 2002). Some of the students in the AWLP study had been learning Welsh intermittently for over 20 years and, in one case, for more than 30 years. They often had a chequered career of learning Welsh, most having attended several courses in the past.

One can only speculate whether this pattern is typical of learners generally, or whether those who are willing to participate in a longitudinal study are more committed to the language despite repeated hindrances over a long period. However, anecdotal evidence and my experience as a practitioner would indicate that this is a common phenomenon, as students often let slip inadvertently that they have attended courses in the past. R. Jones (2005) reports some learners making several attempts at learning before achieving success on an intensive course; other students, however, found that they were unable to make the necessary time commitment required for intensive courses.

Andrea made a comment I have heard many times from L2 students: 'I thought it was going to be easy but it is not'. She attributed her preconceived ideas to advertisements for courses such as Linguaphone which do not allude to the fact that the student will have to expend considerable time and energy to learn an L2. Extravagant claims by publishers and titles such as *Welsh in 3 months* mean that learners become daunted early in the language learning process when experience does not correspond to expectations. Andrea recorded in her dialogue journal that on several occasions she did not have enough Welsh for the 'nitty gritties' of life. She wanted to talk to people about emotional, medical and religious issues too early in her learning and was too ambitious in her aspirations: only nearly fluent learners would be able to sustain conversations of this kind. She had no problems speaking to children, however, and was advised in her dialogue journals to try to hold simpler conversations with adult Welsh-speakers until she had learned more.

S. Thomas, an American of Welsh descent, daunted by private study in the United States, enrolled on an WLPAN in Aberystwyth in 2000. Like Barnes (1997), she soon realised that learning Welsh was not something that happened rapidly, indeed it could well be a lifetime's work and was 'a tough hill to climb alone'. Similarly, Scovel (2000: 4) quotes a student of Tibetan who described his study of the language in a journal as a 'formidable mountain'. Despite his struggles, however, the student hoped that he 'would actually be able to communicate in the language at some point in the future'. The realisation of the time and hard work required to make progress may well play a critical role in decisions to drop out from classes. Learner preparation before classes begin – an issue to be discussed in more depth in the final chapter – could help reduce the disparity between expectations of progress and actual progress.

Time available

Two of the intermediate students, Rees and Roger, were capable of attending an advanced course. However, Rees, who reads Welsh well and has a particularly wide vocabulary, lacks confidence in speaking Welsh. Roger, who has a good command of grammar constructions and a fairly good vocabulary, is also content to remain at intermediate level on account of his busy lifestyle.

Philip explained that over the 30 years he had been studying, there had been many phases when he had conversed regularly in Welsh with his family and other friends and acquaintances. However, he had been unable to sustain his good intentions for very long, partly because – as with other activities such as learning a musical instrument – he was not able to keep up the regular commitment and also because he did not always feel supported in the community or find classes where he felt comfortable. Other students attributed their chequered language learning career to time pressures, the lack of opportunity to practise in Cardiff, having a baby, moving house, changing job, and bereavement.

All the participants in the study were busy people, caring for families and with responsible full or part-time jobs. Even Agnes and Philip, who were retired, had little spare time. Agnes took responsibility for her grandchildren and Philip was involved in many other activities. Some students, such as Clare, travelled a long distance to work and this had implications for the time available to study. Cathy, Sharon and Rees both attributed their lack of practice to laziness as well as their busy lives at work and home. However, the problem would appear to go deeper than laziness: since these are conscientious people, the issues of diffidence when using the language discussed in Chapter 5 may also play a part.

Participants with children in Welsh school or with a Welsh-speaking partner were theoretically at an advantage: even if the family spoke very little Welsh to them, they were exposed to the language at home, reducing the need to go out to seek Welsh-speakers in the community. In practice, however, unless a strategy is agreed, the use of Welsh within the family may become crowded out; and there is also the problem that children are sometimes reluctant to speak to parents in an L2, as in Roger's case, described in Chapter 3. In addition, as noted in earlier chapters, there is often a disinclination to speak in an L2 to a close family member if this means changing the established language of the home.

Davies (2006) reported that many questionnaire respondents in her study of learners' experiences using Welsh indicated that lack of time was a problem. She suggested that tutors should endeavour to incorporate the Welsh language into activities already ongoing in the students' lives, such as sport, music or activities with children. The tutor should be looking for opportunities to direct each student as an individual into what would be helpful for them. It may even be worth setting individual, rather than class, homework for students who are not beginners. Many tutors are, of course, pursuing this route but it may not be possible for students to find suitable Welsh-speakers in their immediate locality, particularly if their interests are not mainstream.

Opportunity

There will always be fewer opportunities for the learner to practise a lesser used language, such as Welsh, than a majority language, such as English. In Cardiff, for instance, Welsh is not a community language, but more a language of networking, so it was especially difficult for the participants in the AWLP to find opportunities to practise, particularly when their busy lifestyles were taken into account. Laura, who lived in a Welsh heartland area before coming to Cardiff, said she had previously practised in shops there but such opportunities were very rare in Cardiff. The learners recorded in their journals that opportunities to use the language in the community were limited. This was a particular problem for Alice who recorded:

> I am learning Welsh for pleasure, as an intellectual challenge and to learn more about this country adjacent to that of my birth. I do not *need* to learn Welsh for any particular professional or personal reason. I think these factors go some way towards explaining why I have difficulty in finding opportunities to practise speaking, listening and reading Welsh. I am new to Cardiff. I have no Welsh-based hobbies, and I do not encounter the language in use in any natural part of my existing home or work routine. (. . .) Ideally, I need an interesting (possibly bilingual) activity that I can take a family member to also. We've just started horse-riding lessons together, for example, but I don't think any of the instructors would want to teach me in Welsh!

Tutors agreed that, despite the increase in the number of Welsh-speakers in Cardiff in recent years, the absence of a Welsh-speaking social circle is a real problem for learners. As Helen Prosser (2002) comments: 'Some people can metamorphose and change their social circle and the language of their home but this is rare'. The younger the learner or the newer to the area, the easier it is to build up a social circle of Welsh-speaking friends. Even Sioned, one of the younger participants, said it was difficult to build up a Welsh-speaking social circle: she had so many friends already in the city who spoke only English, it was difficult to sustain two social orbits. In contrast, a finalist in the learner of the year competition living in a particularly Anglicised area reports success in regularly using Welsh, despite having no Welsh-speaking family or friends when she started learning. However, she realised that to do so, the learner had to be particularly proactive in finding opportunities (Morgan, 2002). Gwen Awbery offered a Welsh-speaker's perspective on this issue:

> It is difficult for Welsh-speakers to have opportunities to use Welsh in Cardiff and when they get together they may find it particularly stressful to have to accommodate learners. I would have to change my lifestyle completely if I wanted to speak more Welsh on a regular basis. Time is a factor for native speakers as well as learners.

Conclusion

Time and opportunity, then, are problems not easily solved. The learner who wishes to progress to fluency has to be very determined to overcome the obstacles discussed in earlier chapters, particularly in an area where Welsh is not a community language.

As indicated earlier, practising with one or two native speakers may initially be sufficient. Learners need to either find such a person or an interest such as a choir, a sports club, a church, or a public house where Welsh can be practised. As well as working on the linguistic skills in class and overcoming problems that arise in the community, learners need good time management skills and the resolve to seek out opportunities to use Welsh outside class. It is hard work and requires stamina and determination. In the light of the problems discussed in this and previous chapters, learners have to be highly motivated to continue learning and using Welsh. I will discuss motivation in more detail in Chapter 7.

Chapter 7
Sustaining Motivation

Introduction

It is evident from the foregoing discussion that a strong driving force is essential if learners are to sustain their initial motivation to learn, for, as Rogers (1992: 28) comments: 'lack of or wilting motivation is one of the main reasons why learning fails'. In the preceding chapters, I have discussed barriers both internal and external to the learner that may cause Welsh and other L2 learners to become less motivated to learn and use the target language. In this chapter, the focus will be on motivation for – rather than obstacles to – successful language learning. A brief review of the literature on the role of motivation in language learning will provide a context for discussion of two key questions in relation to the present study: Who are the adult learners of Welsh? and, What are the motives of adults for learning the language?

Motivation of L2 Learners

Research on language learners' motivations has been influenced for almost half a century by the work of Gardner and colleagues in Canada who argued that motivation was as important as linguistic aptitude for the successful acquisition of a second language (Clément & Gardner, 2001; Gardner, 1985; Gardner & Lambert, 1959, 1972; Gardner & MacIntyre, 1991; Tremblay & Gardner, 1995). These scholars brought social-psychological perspectives to bear on the development of a theory of motivation based on scientific, empirical data. A distinction was made between *integrative* orientation towards the study of a second language – when the aim was to learn more about the language group and identify with that society – and the *instrumental* orientation when the reasons were of more utilitarian value, such as better positions at work or better education. In earlier studies of French Canadian learners, it was the integratively orientated students who were generally the most successful, had the more favourable attitudes towards members of the French group and were more strongly motivated to acquire their language (Gardner & Lambert, 1959, 1972).

An escalation in L2 motivation studies in the 1990s was described by Gardner and Tremblay (1994) as a 'motivational renaissance' as researchers began expanding the concept of L2 learning motivation beyond the original model by including concepts such as intrinsic-extrinsic motivation, hierarchies of need (from safety to self-actualisation), need for achievement, social context, expectancy of success and direction of causality (see, for instance, Crookes & Schmidt, 1991; Dörnyei, 1998, 2001a; Oxford & Shearin, 1994). The current view is that there is no longer reason to argue that strong motivation is driven only by integrative factors (Gardner, 2001; Tremblay & Gardner, 1995). More recent developments are characterised by a move towards a more situated approach, examining how the immediate learning context influences the learners' overall disposition and how motivation affects learning processes in class. This approach has led to increased attention to the dynamic character and temporal variation of motivation. Shoaib and Dörnyei (2004), for instance, argue that there is a need to adopt an approach that can account for the daily 'ups and downs' of motivation to learn, that is, the ongoing changes of motivation over time.

There was evidence of fluctuating motivation in the AWLP. For instance, as indicated in Chapter 3, when commenting on the tendency for his interlocutors to switch languages when he attempted to use French in France and Welsh in Wales, Alan wondered why he had put so much effort into learning. His initial high motivation to become a second language speaker sank almost to the point of making him want to give up altogether. Other students expressed similar sentiments but did not view the attitudes of the native speakers as insurmountable problems; some, such as Cathy, recognised that many native speakers were diffident about their own Welsh skills and others, such as Philip and Kim, gradually developed strategies enabling them to be more in control in such situations.

In terms of the two types of motivation highlighted in the original Gardner model, integrative motivation certainly dominates in this study as all the AWLP students apart from Clare indicated that their main motivation was integrative and even Clare, whose main motivation was related to her employment prospects, also expressed the desire to integrate with Welsh-speakers. However, the two types of motivation are not mutually exclusive, can co-exist in an individual and can change over time. There may be instrumental components alongside integrative motivations and there are often integrative elements to instrumental motivation. For example, a Welsh learner whose decision to study was triggered by a desire to communicate with a family member or significant other may be spurred on to fluency by the instrumental motive, as the language is used increasingly in the workplace. On the other hand, students learning in the workplace may find that they use Welsh more in the community than at work and their main motivation becomes that of communicating with Welsh-speakers. In some instances, it may not be clear which motivation was the original one. Moreover, the strengths of both kinds of motivation are likely to be different in different contexts – for example, for Jews returning to Israel, both instrumental and integrative motivation might be expected to be stronger than for any Welsh learner because of heightened cultural, religious and political issues (Newcombe & Newcombe, 2001a). Whereas the usual tendency has been to view motives as affecting behaviour, this can be a two-way process (Baker & Prys Jones, 1998: 652). As students become competent in an L2, integrative and instrumental may fluctuate according to how successful they perceive themselves to be when performing a linguistic activity. As Ehrman (1996: 141) points out:

> Another important element of motivation is that it is sensitive to success and failure. If one succeeds at a task, he or she is usually energised to do it some more. On the other hand, failure may lead to avoidance of the challenge. (For some, failure may lead to redoubled effort, but only temporarily.)

This principle is arguably even more relevant in the community than in the classroom, given that anxiety may be more strongly aroused by speaking than by learning, as indicated in Chapter 5 (see MacIntyre, 1995).

For the purposes of the AWLP, we were not examining in detail the types of motivation but endeavouring to find ways to augment and sustain whatever motivation exists.

Who Are the Adult Welsh Learners?

In relation to the present study, an understanding of *who* Welsh adult learners are gives useful indications as to their motivation for learning. They appear to be a very heterogeneous group. Their rapid growth in numbers has mirrored a similar development in Welsh-medium education for children.

Parents wishing to support their children are by no means the only adult learners. Griffiths (2001), for instance, reports on learners in the political domain such as Jane Davidson, David Davies and the late Phil Williams, who have used Welsh confidently when speaking at the Welsh Assembly Government (WAG). Janet Ryder from the North of England, now a fluent second language Welsh-speaker, and an assembly member for *Plaid Cymru*, the Welsh Nationalist party, is also a keen Welsh language advocate (Ryder, 2004). Similarly, the veteran Welsh language campaigner and former president of *Plaid Cymru*, the late Gwynfor Evans (1912–2005) learned Welsh as a teenager and his successor, Dafydd Wigley was born in Derby, England.

Many learners have made important contributions to Welsh cultural life. For instance, Robat Powell, a Welsh learner from Ebbw Vale (Jenkins, 1999: 382), won the chair at the National Eisteddfod, a high profile and much coveted prize, for writing an ode in *cynghanedd*. Alison Layland, a learner from England, has won prizes for short stories and has published a Welsh language novel (Layland, 2004). Lois Arnold, winner of the Learner of the Year competition in 2004 has published a novel for learners (Arnold, 2004). In 2005, Christine James, who learned Welsh as an L2 in school, won the crown for the best poem, another highly coveted prize, at the National Eisteddfod (Davies, 2005b). Interestingly, some of the iconic figures of modern Welsh-speaking Wales have worked on their Welsh language skills as adults and have been learners, they are people who almost lost their Welsh or were brought up in England. These include some highly regarded literary figures such as Waldo Williams, Saunders Lewis, Emyr Humphreys, and R.S. Thomas.

While most WfA students originate in Wales, some are in-migrants from other parts of the United Kingdom and elsewhere. A radio programme for learners, *Catchphrase*, for instance, featured Beverley Lennon from South London whose family originates from Jamaica and who subsequently went on to teach Welsh as a second language and had her own show on the Welsh-medium radio channel, BBC *Radio Cymru* (Unidentified, 1999a). Morris (2000b) comments that it is no longer unusual to meet Welsh-speaking people born in other countries or members of ethnic minorities, who often have had little prior contact with traditional Welsh cultural domains. This diversity is reflected in the many Cardiff learners whose origins are overseas (Unidentified, 1999b). There has been a fundamental change in attitude since C. Williams (1997: 30) wrote of her childhood experiences in the 1950s and 1960s in North Wales when she claims: 'there was no conception of black Welsh'. As indicated in Chapter 4, some in-migrants are eager not only to learn the language but to imbibe the culture of their adopted country; this is the case for students from overseas as well as other parts of the United Kingdom.

Many learners in retirement have grandchildren in Welsh-medium education. Some have finally found time to fulfil a lifelong dream in learning their ancestral language while others, many of whom are in-migrants, wish to integrate with Welsh-speakers. The popular belief that it is better to learn a second language early and that older learners are disadvantaged is a hotly debated topic (Singleton, 2001). The fact remains, however, that adults with high motivation and a positive attitude to learning an L2 can learn well and speedily. Baker and Prys Jones (1998: 659) point to the case of Den and Ann Rees, who after early retirement in Gwent, one of the most Anglicised areas of Wales, and attendance on an *WLPAN* course became fluent Welsh-speakers, changing the language of their home from English to Welsh despite no family or educational background in the Welsh language. They now express themselves more fluently in Welsh than some native Welsh-speakers. Their experience demonstrates that age need not be a significant factor in second language learning, at least for some learners. Factors such as motivation, perseverance, commitment, and opportunities to practice play a significant role, as do personality and WTC. Another remarkable example of an older learner is Hilda Hunter, a professional musician from Aberystwyth, who began learning Welsh in the year 2000 when she was over 80 years old, attained fluency and published her autobiography in Welsh (Hunter, 2006).

Celebrities from a variety of walks of life have been amongst the Welsh learners who have proliferated during the latter half of the 20th century. Within Wales, famous Welsh learners include sportsmen Nigel Walker and Mark Aizelwood, actress Ruth Madoc, sportswoman Tanni Grey-Thompson, the newsreader Sara Edwards, the meteorologist Derek Brockway and the journalist, Janet Street-Porter. An example from outside Wales is the English actress, Stephanie Cole who reports learning Welsh in 1972 (Cole, 1998; Duncan, 1998), when her aim was to read and appreciate the works of Dafydd ap Gwilym, whom she regards as the Welsh Shakespeare. The astronaut, Dafydd Rhys Williams, born in Canada but with roots in South Wales, was able to send a Welsh language message from Space (Jenkins, 1999: 436).

A significant proportion of WfA tutors are second language Welsh-speakers (Krashner & Taylor, 1992). Lila Haines, originally from Ireland (Unidentified, 1998b: 11) speaks for many adult tutors, who are second language speakers: 'I believe that learners can make very good teachers because we know what difficulties are facing people who are learning'. Similarly, Angela Evans (2004), originally from the North of England comments: 'I find that my own experiences of learning the language help me to appreciate the difficulties my pupils experience. I have learned not to take anything for granted, and to put myself in their shoes'. Empathy with students is likely to reduce anxiety not only in the classroom but outside because the adult learner who becomes a tutor has successfully transferred from the L2 classroom to the community and should therefore be able to motivate students to do likewise (Arnold & Brown, 1999: 19).

WfA learners thus come from many different starting points: they include parents of children in Welsh-medium education; politicians and people wishing to take part in Welsh cultural life; and celebrities. In many cases, they fall into two or more of these categories. Their motivation for learning is likely to have been predominantly integrative rather than instrumental. In some cases, they have gone on to become teachers of Welsh for adults, their own experience of learning making them well-placed to empathise with – and motivate – other learners. Those who become tutors may not necessarily be exhibiting instrumental motivation. The majority of tutors are part-time and view their activities as an extension of their desire to integrate in the Welsh community.

Various sources give us an insight into the reasons why adults have begun to learn Welsh over the last four decades and these are discussed now.

The Motives of Adults Learning Welsh

Media

One of the earliest studies (Williams, 1965) indicated that interest in following news and other television programmes was one of the most important motivations, reflecting the increasing importance of media in people's lives during that period. The ability to follow the media is given as a motivation for learning the language by relatively few people in an early study (Hughes, 1989) but is more prominent in all subsequent studies. Newcombe (2002c) for instance, reports that the wish to read Welsh literature and follow the media was strongly associated with successful outcome (defined as using Welsh at least three times a week after completing a course). Similarly, learners and potential learners interviewed for the WCC study (R. Jones, 2005) indicated they would like to follow the media in Welsh, although this was not the main motivator for learning. Interestingly, Davies (2006) also reports that listening to the radio, television or webcasts came high on the list of factors helping fluent learners to maintain their Welsh by supplying naturalistic listening practice. Some of the respondents who gave this answer specifically stated that it helped their understanding of different accents and dialects – one of the problems described by learners in the AWLP project and in the literature on learners discussed in Chapter 3. Though following the media may not be an initial motivator, it may help in sustaining motivation: it is a non-threatening way for the learner to acquire language for use at a later date with native speakers.

Regaining a family language

Her Majesty's Inspectors (HMI) (1984: 13–14) report that, prominent in almost every class of adults learning Welsh, were those seeking to regain a language not transmitted to them by a previous generation. Hughes (1989), however, reports a sharp drop in those wishing to restore a parental language. Similarly, in Newcombe's (2002c) study, only 27 out of 175 students in Cardiff chose the restoration of a parental language as a motivator, and only six of these considered it a main motivator (Newcombe, 2002c). Yet, as indicated in Chapter 4, in each focus group held for the WCC study (R. Jones, 2005), there was at least one person who was partly motivated by wishing to regain a family language that had not been transmitted, usually in order to be more involved in Welsh culture.

Integration with Welsh-speakers

Integration with Welsh-speakers – family and/or friends – figures high in all the motivational studies undertaken in Wales. This is usually linked with a desire to preserve the language and an awareness that, if living in Wales, one should speak Welsh and, to a lesser degree, take an interest in Welsh culture. Gareth Kiff, a senior tutor at Cardiff University has observed that the most successful learners are usually those who desire not only to integrate with Welsh-speakers but also have a keen interest in Welsh culture. He views an interest in the media and Welsh culture as a distinct advantage to sustaining initial motivation to learn, as the need to understand the culture and the whole concept of Welshness makes learning the language more authentic. HMI (1984) makes reference to learners attending bridging courses in order to achieve their goals of communicating in Welsh and appreciating Welsh culture.

Others also provide support for this position. J.P. Davies (1986), studying the motivations of learners in Clwyd, North East Wales, concluded that the skills most important to learners were communication with other Welsh-speakers, whether family, friends, or social contacts, and that the main motivation was to speak Welsh because of living in Wales. In a national study of learners in 1987, the most important motives were generally associated with integration and identity (Hughes, 1989). A study of an WLPAN course in Bangor by J.J. Williams (1994: 54) demonstrated that the prime reasons for learning Welsh were linked with the desire to communicate with friends, an interest in Wales and Welsh culture, and the sense of being 'duty bound' to learn the language of their country of residence.

A study of the 1993/4 WLPAN at the Welsh Language Teaching Centre, Cardiff (Newcombe, 1995), indicated that the integrative motive dominated (Newcombe & Newcombe, 2001a). In a later study of students from the Welsh Language Teaching Centre, it emerged in a follow-up study that students with integrative orientation were more likely to continue using Welsh (Newcombe, 2002c).

Studies in Swansea and the surrounding area also revealed the prevalence of the integrative motive. The linguistic characteristics of the area of residence may, however, be more important than the birthplace of the learner, as those living in Welsh-speaking areas viewed learning of the language as a way of integrating into the community more readily than those who lived in more Anglicised areas (Morris, 1996, 1997, 2000a, 2000b, 2001).

Davidson and Piette (2000) concluded from evaluation forms and students' interviews at Bangor, North Wales, that motivation for learning Welsh was linked with issues of integration, inclusion, and identity. R. Jones (2005) also revealed the dominance of the integrative motive amongst adult Welsh learners in all areas of Wales, with speaking to family and friends being the predominant reason for learning.

Children in Welsh-medium education

An increasingly prevalent motivator from the mid-eighties with learners between the ages of 25 and 45 was to help children attending Welsh school, reflecting the growth in Welsh-medium schools during this period (Hughes, 1989). Students motivated to help children and grandchildren also figured in Newcombe's studies (1995, 2002c) and in the studies in Swansea and the surrounding areas (Morris, 1996, 1997, 2000a, 2000b, 2001). Newcombe (2002c) was also able to demonstrate that having children in Welsh school was strongly associated with successful outcome. The presence of children in the household also had an impact on people's willingness to learn Welsh (R. Jones, 2005). Almost one in four people with children in the household are currently learning or would like to learn Welsh, compared to one in six of those without children. Tutors interviewed were not surprised at this finding, stressing that, as parents, learners have opportunities to build on what they learn in class in the home and school contexts on a regular basis. Helen Prosser (2002), then Director of Teaching at the Cardiff Centre for Adults Learning Welsh, draws attention to the importance of parents learning before their children attend nursery and school, so that language can be reinforced in the home, pointing out that it is often difficult to switch if the parent becomes fluent later. Her own children and others often refuse to speak Welsh to a person whom they have previously associated with English when the person attempts to switch.

Quite a large number of my students embarked on learning the language in order to support their children, helping them with their school work and being able to discuss progress with teachers. Many report that they may well have given up learning had it not been for such a well-defined goal. Sustained motivation of this kind has also been recorded elsewhere. For instance, Comings *et al.* (2000) found that students learning

English as a second language who mentioned the goal of supporting their children were more likely to persist.

Instrumental motivation

HMI (1984) reports that learners studying for professional and occupational reasons were found everywhere but particularly in the North and North West, where many were sponsored by their employers. In a study of the 1993/4 WLPAN at the Welsh Language Teaching Centre, Cardiff (Newcombe, 1995), 39 out of 74 students reported instrumental motivation but only 11 students reported instrumental motivation alone (Newcombe & Newcombe, 2001a). In a later study of students from the Welsh Language Teaching Centre and other providers in Cardiff, only 2 out of 208 respondents indicated instrumental motivation alone (Newcombe, 2002c); and students with instrumental motivation were less likely to still be using Welsh at follow-up. Studies in Swansea and the surrounding area confirmed that instrumental was less powerful than integrative motivation. Surprisingly perhaps, there was a greater tendency to see Welsh as an employment asset by students in more Anglicised areas (Morris 1996, 1997, 2000a, 2000b, 2001). R. Jones (2005) reported strong evidence that learners and potential learners would like to be able to use Welsh in workplace settings, on the high street and when using public facilities, although these were rarely the main motive for learning. There is substantial anecdotal evidence that many learners able to sustain conversations in Welsh lack the confidence necessary to use the language in the workplace. Pamela Marsden (2001), for instance, uses Welsh regularly in the community but lacks confidence to do so at work. Indeed, using Welsh in the workplace or in the business domain is often viewed by learners as a particularly high accomplishment. Greenslade (1992: 34), a fluent L2 Welsh-speaker wrote:

> Go on
> Write a cheque in IT
> A couple of seconds
> And it will all be over
> Then you can get on
> With the rest of your life . . .

Significantly, when Petro (1997: 316) wrote a cheque in IT (Welsh) in the bank in Patagonia, as there was no other language of communication, she regarded her success in this domain as a marker of great progress: 'When you can use Welsh at the bank you know you've made it'.

Motivation on intensive residential courses

C. Jones (1991) studied 40 learners on the summer residential WLPAN in Lampeter in 1989 and, although conceding that no definitive conclusions could be drawn from this small sample, notes that the feeling of belonging to a nation, identity, and a sense of duty to learn Welsh were the prime motivators. This course normally includes students from overseas, who are usually learning because they have a Welsh family background, or in some cases, because they speak another Celtic language. A high proportion of those attending the Lampeter course are full-time students. Consequently, more students wished to learn in order to study literature and fewer to help children at Welsh schools than in the Hughes National Survey (1989). Relatively few respondents reported a Welsh-speaking family as a significant motivator. However, in Newcombe's (2002c) study of the 1999 Lampeter course, though integration and preservation of the language were the key motivators, 9 out of 19 respondents had been partly motivated because of Welsh being an ancestral language, and four reported this as their main motivation.

In an ethnographic study of the 2001 Lampeter WLPAN, Lewis (2001) notes that the learners were mainly integratively motivated and those students who indicated an instrumental motivation also reported integrative elements. As Lewis observes, whatever the nature of their motivation, only highly motivated, dedicated individuals will commit time and money to such an intensive course. The same explanation was suggested by Newcombe (1995) for the high response rate to questionnaires and the positive comments received when the less intensive WLPAN in Cardiff was evaluated.

Learners without Welsh roots

Lewis (2001) observes that some of the overseas learners were 'lone wolves' and did not really fall into any category. It is difficult to categorise motivations of students from overseas, particularly those with no family background in the language. Pam Petro, whose background is Hungarian and German, has no Welsh connections. In response to friends' and relatives' questions about her reasons for studying Welsh at Harvard and spending a summer vacation on an intensive Welsh course in Lampeter, she explains:

> I don't know. Maybe when I first went to Wales and unwittingly enrolled in an English department the old Welsh god of irony vowed to teach me a lesson and made me besotted with the place and its language (I made up the god of Irony but there really is an old Celtic god of panic, who

comes in handy in cases of both travel and language study). To tell the truth, I really can't say why my desire to continue learning Welsh got so out of hand that I chose to pursue it on a five-month, fourteen-country crusade around the world. Perhaps I had a premonition of what Ursula Imadegawa would tell me in Tokyo. 'Pam', she said ... 'you only regret what you don't do' (Petro, 1997: 4).

Other comments from Petro (1997: 78) suggest that motivation was linked with identity issues, as discussed in Chapter 4.

Motivation to use in specialised areas

If the motives of some overseas learners are unclear, even less obvious are those of Turner (1976), a scientist from England, who persuaded one of his students to learn Welsh with him. They translated their work on microbiology into Welsh, coining new expressions for terms such as 'heterokaryon test'. Turner had no Welsh connections and, though repeatedly asked why he learned the language, was unable to give an adequate answer. Inspired by reading George Borrow's *Wild Wales*, he taught himself in Bristol and, when he moved to Wales, continued to learn from television and literature. He became increasingly concerned as he witnessed English people moving into Welsh-speaking areas and Welsh-speakers turning to English and using English with their children. Turner is an example of someone who was obviously integratively motivated and – because of his love of Wales, its heritage and culture – strove to promote all things Welsh in as many spheres as possible, even the most atypical. A more recent example of specialised motivation is Robert Newcombe's translation of the Excel spreadsheet into Welsh (Newcombe & Soto, 2006).

As Welsh is being used increasingly in the workplace since the passing of the 1993 Welsh Language Act, efforts have been made to coin and in some cases standardise terms in the business world and in specialist fields such as law, science, and dentistry (E.J. Hughes, 2005; Lewis, 1992). Subjects such as education, administration, human resources, legislation, retail terminology, shop signs, food menus, finance, and highways are included in the Welsh National Database of Terms, downloadable from the Welsh Language Board's website. As time goes by, more and more specialised terms will be provided with Welsh equivalents by Welsh language experts obviating the need for the creation of terms by the scientific specialists. Interestingly, unlike other European languages which generally use American English for media and computer terminology, Welsh has coined its own words for television, computer, internet, website, and mobile phone. In 2006, the WLB launched a glossary for the IT generation that includes words for all essential IT usage such as cookies, interactive white board and laptop. In addition, a trial period for predictive texting in Welsh was launched in 2006. The texting software predicts Welsh words as the text is written and is suitable for everybody with a phone with internet access. It is hoped that developments such as these will help normalise Welsh in the workplace and aid native speakers and learners alike.

Learners outside Wales

Sustaining motivation to use the language outside Wales is difficult as two American participants on the Lampeter intensive course testify. Trosset (2002) last used Welsh when in Australia in 1995. Petro (2002) uses spoken Welsh only very occasionally in the United States. Lewis (1999), who learned Welsh in New Zealand in the 1980s, reports that appointment to a responsible lecturing post meant that her Welsh studies could not continue. She now has no one with whom to practise and her use of Welsh is limited to the occasional singing of Welsh hymns and when visiting Wales (Lewis, 2003).

Branches of *CYD* have been established overseas to enable learners to meet and use Welsh with fluent speakers. Many overseas learners, of course, have no access to *CYD*. Bohren (2006) bemoans the fact that he no longer speaks Welsh in the United States despite attaining a high degree of fluency and giving the inaugural address at the opening of the Learners' tent at the 1978 National Eisteddfod. Had he settled in a large city such as Boston rather than in a thinly-populated rural area, he believes there would have been opportunities to maintain his fluency because of the greater availability of Welsh-speakers. In contrast, an example of an actively fluent learner overseas is Kevin Rottet, a linguist from Wisconsin, who learned so successfully he was invited to teach Welsh on the *Cwrs Madog*, a week-long intensive Welsh course held annually in a variety of venues in the United States (McCaughey, 2001/2). Chris Cope from Minnesota who learned through the BBC website is another example of a highly-motivated, committed learner in the United States. His efforts to teach himself Welsh have been so successful that Cardiff University offered him a place to study for a BA degree in Welsh in 2006. Cope (2006) stresses the importance of continuing to learn when reaching the inevitable plateaux common to all L2 learners and the value of support from close family members.

Motivation of Students in the AWLP Study

Before participating in the qualitative research, AWLP students completed a questionnaire on which they were asked to tick all motivators that applied to them, and to indicate the two main motivators. Twenty-four areas of motivation were listed. Items 1–19 were integrative, 20–23 were instrumental and 24 an open-ended 'other'. Respondents were asked to tick all that applied to them and to choose the two main ones. All 16 students showed evidence of integrative orientation. Some also expressed instrumental, but this dominated in only one case. Fourteen students selected integrative or a combination of integrative and instrumental, with instrumental as the weaker. One student selected mainly instrumental motives with a weak integrative element and one student selected both integrative and instrumental, choosing one of each as the two main motivations.

Table 7.1 shows the motivations of students in the study. Where instrumental or integrative was ticked on the initial questionnaire but not chosen as one of the main motivators, it is included in the secondary motivation column. It was interesting to note in interviews and focus groups that, as Shoaib and Dörnyei (2004) have suggested, motivation was not static but changeable according to learners' circumstances, confidence levels, and the degree of support received. In addition, instrumental motivation may have been difficult to sustain in some cases with the realisation that accurate communication in the workplace is often crucial, leading to lack of confidence that this could ever be achieved.

In order to interpret the findings of the questionnaires, it is necessary to draw on other data sources. All of the students who had completed the questionnaires had been interviewed for the project; some had also completed journals or dialogue journals. The various influences on their motivation are discussed below.

Media

In the AWLP, the student who expressed most interest in following the media in the long term was Alice, the beginner. As indicated in Chapter 6, Alice was learning Welsh for pleasure and not for any professional reason. Part of that pleasure was to follow Welsh media, both radio and television, and understand more about Welsh culture and politics through the medium of Welsh. This is a clear case of intrinsic motivation and integrative orientation and total lack of instrumental motivation. Rees and Agnes, the two students who were most diffident about practising speaking, were also motivated by a desire to follow the media but their main desire was to be competent readers of the Welsh language in order to read newspapers and magazines in Welsh, as well as books. Again, there is clear evidence of intrinsic motivation and integrative orientation with both these students and, in the case of Rees, very weak instrumental motivation. He indicated when interviewed that he would not have attended a Welsh course if his

Table 7.1 Motivations of students in the AWLP in Cardiff

Student	Level	Main motivation	Secondary motivation	Main motivators on initial questionnaire
Agnes	I	Integrative	None	I want to keep the language alive. I live in Wales and I ought to learn Welsh.
Alan	A	Integrative	Instrumental	I am a Welsh person. My children are attending a Welsh school.
Alice	B	Integrative	None	I like Welsh. I want to understand the media in Welsh and read the Welsh Press.
Andrea*	I	Integrative	None	My children attend a Welsh school. I want to communicate with Welsh-speakers (mainly linked with school).
Cathy	A	Integrative	None	I live in Wales and I ought to learn Welsh. My children attend a Welsh school.
Clare	B	Instrumental	Integrative	Perhaps Welsh will be essential in my work. I want to understand and communicate with Welsh-speakers.
Kim	A	Integrative	None	My children attend a Welsh school. Welsh is my partner's first language.
Laura	B (Int)	Integrative	Instrumental	I want to keep the language alive. I am a Welsh person.
Lydia*	I	Integrative	Instrumental	I want to communicate with Welsh-speakers. Welsh is useful in my work.
Philip*	I	Integrative	None	I want to speak to my family in Welsh. I live in Wales and I ought to learn Welsh.

(Continued)

Table 7.1 (Continued)

Student	Level	Main motivation	Secondary motivation	Main motivators on initial questionnaire
Ray[†]	B	Integrative	Instrumental	I live in Wales and I ought to learn Welsh. Other – All of my wife's family and my children are Welsh-speaking.
Rees	I	Integrative	Instrumental	I want to keep the language alive. Other – I am interested in history and language.
Roger	I	Integrative	Instrumental	I want to keep the language alive. I am a Welsh person.
Sally[†]	A	Integrative	None	I like Welsh. I have friends who speak Welsh.
Sioned	I	Integrative	None	I want to use Welsh in my home with my family. I want to understand and communicate with Welsh-speakers.
Sharon[*]	I	Integrative	None	My children attend Welsh school. I want to keep the language alive.

A – Advanced   I – Intermediate   B – Beginner   (Int) – Intensive.
[*]These students wrote dialogue journals.
[†]These students were interviewed but did not write journals.

employer had not pressed him into enrolling as he was quite content to learn on his own through books and was far more interested to develop reading and writing rather than speaking skills.

Regaining a family language

There was no strong motivation to regain the language of parents and grandparents. Sioned's father and grandmother are fluent speakers but this was not a particularly significant motivator for her. However, some students were indeed motivated to become fluent in the language of one's ancestors, albeit several generations in the past. Kim, from England said: 'I feel I have a lot of Welsh blood'. Likewise Roger insisted vehemently: '*Cymro dw i*' [I am a Welshman], though he was born and brought up in England. National identity is such a complicated issue and is often difficult to attribute in individual cases. Such motivations were also linked with liking the language and wanting to make a contribution to its preservation.

Integration with Welsh-speakers

Most participants identified the desire to communicate with friends and family, or a significant other, as a particularly significant motive for learning. Lydia, in contrast, explained that even though she said she would like to communicate with Welsh-speakers, her main concern was to understand what was being said so that she would not be excluded. Clare, whose main trigger was the instrumental motive, found that the desire to integrate with Welsh-speakers and other learners had flourished since she began learning.

Children in Welsh-medium education

The desire to speak to children was particularly in evidence. Parents such as Alan, Roger, Cathy, Sharon, Andrea, and Kim felt it was important for their children that they should know as much Welsh as possible. Sharon wished to keep one step ahead of her children – a baby and a toddler – in Welsh and to be able to speak to her children's school teachers from the beginning. She was originally concerned with keeping the language alive, liking the language and integrating with Welsh-speakers, but having children had provided even stronger motivation to learn. Kim's experience is similar: she wants Welsh to be 'more real' for her children and 'to be second nature to them'. She is aware of the danger, for instance, that, if children speak Welsh only at school, they may lose the language when they leave. Clare, who started learning for instrumental reasons, is now eager to help her children, who though attending English-medium schools, participate in *Eisteddfodau* by reciting and singing. Philip is the only person in his family who does not speak Welsh fluently. His concern that, if grandchildren come, he will be the only family member who cannot converse freely with them has increased his motivation. Laura indicated that, if she were to have children, she would want them to attend Welsh school.

Instrumental motivation and the workplace

Workplace Welsh is now a particular area of growth in WfA. In settings other than education, this is, however, a recent development, particularly in the more Anglicised areas of Wales, which has, as yet, received little attention from researchers. Williams and Morris (2000: 150) are certainly correct in arguing that a link exists between the struggle to establish Welsh as the language of work and the increase in its prestige value. The views of the AWLP students on the use of Welsh in the workplace are therefore illuminating in this respect; so, too, were interview data from tutors with experience of teaching Welsh in this setting.

At the focus group attended by Alan, Agnes, Cathy, Kim, and Rees, students were unanimous that the use of Welsh in the workplace needed to be approached with caution, reflecting a deep-seated fear of making a mistake about crucial arrangements. Alan, for instance, stressed that, as the nature of his work involved decisions about people's lives, caution was needed when using an L2. Similar issues occurred in other settings, such as making arrangements for collecting young children; as there is more chance of misunderstanding when using an L2, there was general agreement that anything of vital importance expressed in Welsh should be repeated in English as a precaution.

At another focus group, three of the students – Andrea, Sharon and Philip – were positive about use of Welsh in the workplace. It became apparent during discussion, however, that it was the educational orbit in which they felt they could build confidence to use their Welsh; as all had experience of Welsh-medium nurseries and schools, this observation was not surprising. In contrast, the other two members of the group, Alice and Sioned, were adamant that they would not use Welsh in their workplace setting, apart from socialising with colleagues, as they would be too anxious that a misunderstanding would arise. Alice pointed to the technical nature of her work and the fact that many of the terms in regular use have no equivalent in Welsh. Sioned explained that native speakers and learners alike are reluctant to admit to a knowledge of the language as they may be called upon by their managers to act as spokespeople on the media. They regard themselves as inadequate for this task, which would be an added pressure on their time in a busy working environment. However, like several other participants, she was happy to use Welsh socially at work.

Clare was the only student for whom the main motivational trigger had been instrumental: her employer wanted her to learn Welsh. In fact, she believed she had been appointed to her present post because she had some knowledge of Welsh and expressed a willingness to develop further. One of her main responsibilities was to promote Welsh in the institution and she was aware that, in the future, there might be closer links with NAfW, making her knowledge of Welsh particularly useful. She thought that her future employment opportunities might also be enhanced by pursuing her Welsh studies.

Interestingly, some students working in a Welsh environment indicated that their main motivation was not instrumental. Rees for example, whose line manager was particularly eager for him to converse in Welsh, was more interested in reading Welsh history and cultural affairs than in using Welsh at the office. Similarly, Laura, who at the time of the study worked in the Museum of Welsh Life in Cardiff, displayed powerful integrative motivation and was eager to defend her Welsh identity and contribute to preserving Welsh language and culture. Her post in Wales was temporary but she gave up an opportunity for a permanent job in England in order to learn the language. However, a desire to preserve the Welsh language and to use it socially with friends and colleagues is very important to her.

Roger thought that Welsh could be useful in his work in the future. He indicated that, though he is officially encouraged to learn Welsh by his employer, he is often required to be involved in work activities at the time of the lessons. This is a common problem in workplace classes and frequently bemoaned by students and tutors. At work, Roger uses Welsh for pleasantries and 'to set an atmosphere' if he is liaising with organisations like WLB or NAfW. The subject matter he needs to discuss in these situations is complex and he lacks the necessary confidence. His main motivation is linked with preserving the language, his strong sense of Welsh identity and the desire to use Welsh in the family, socially, and at cultural events. Reading Welsh literature in the original is also an important long-term goal as he believes that a great deal is lost in translation.

Wider issues for Welsh in the workplace

Tutors also threw light on questions of motivation in relation to the use of Welsh in the workplace. Gareth Kiff, a senior tutor in Cardiff, for instance, observed that instrumental motivation in learners sponsored by employers is often not high. They often do not want a window into another culture and are usually not as successful as learners who are eager to imbibe Welsh culture and socialise with Welsh-speakers. These learners frequently do not strive beyond their employer's requirements. Gwen Awbery, an experienced tutor/organiser for WfA, made a similar point drawing attention to a noticeable drop-out rate in students driven only by instrumental motives in her classes. She attributes this to the fact that home and school contexts are more likely to provide regular opportunities for practice than many workplaces.

Anxieties about workplace Welsh are not limited to the linguistic. As a practitioner, I have observed that daytime courses specifically for workplace groups can produce tensions for individuals of mixed status as well as mixed ability and those in senior positions may feel threatened when junior colleagues perform better in class. In addition, work commitments often result in poor attendance and slow progress.

Promoting Welsh in the business world is probably best seen as a long-term venture, focusing first on native speakers and advanced learners and only later on beginners. The anxieties of native speakers about their levels of proficiency in the language have already been discussed at length (see, in particular, Chapters 1 and 3). In the work place, preconceptions about the suitability of Welsh in official and business domains may also serve as an obstacle to the use of the language in the work place. It is a myth, however, that some languages are unable to accommodate to new domains, such as the commercial or scientific (Harlow, 1998). It is also worth noting here that in the Norman and Mediaeval periods Welsh was used extensively in the business and legal system (Evans, 2000; R.O. Jones, 1999). This, incidentally, is another area that could be usefully dealt with at learner' preparation courses.

Given the increased demand for work-related courses from native speakers as well as from fluent learners, it could be expedient to concentrate on this target group rather than beginners. One way of addressing the concerns identified above about the importance of accuracy in decision making, for instance in fields which affect safety, would be to offer specialised language training for specific professions. Because of the relatively small numbers involved, these would need to be organised on a national rather than a local level.

If even fluent speakers experience anxiety in relation to the use of Welsh in the work place, the concerns of less advanced learners are easy to understand. In the early stages, it may be unrealistic to expect Welsh to be used for reasons other than socialising with colleagues. When a network of Welsh-speakers in the workplace is in operation, opportunities for practice are likely to increase. However, it is worth noting that in some work place settings, accuracy is not always essential. First-language Welsh-speakers, for instance, often value hospital staff who use some Welsh, even if their knowledge is not sufficiently advanced to discuss medical issues (G.W. Roberts, 1994). Likewise, Barnes (1997), a social worker who learned Welsh as an adult, found that her knowledge of Welsh, though limited, was a great comfort to a Welsh-speaking family, who found difficulty expressing themselves in English.

Commitment on the part of the employer is vital. Often, lip service is paid to encouraging employees to develop Welsh skills and, when pressures increase, students are unable to attend as employers insist they give priority to work. Even when there is commitment on the employer's part, however, students whose work necessitates travel away from base frequently have to miss sessions. Particularly high motivation and practical solutions to tackle these problems are essential if learners are to progress under such circumstances. Role models may be helpful in inspiring students; a particularly inspiring role model in North Wales is the chief constable of Gwynedd, Richard Brunstrom, now a fluent second language speaker, who believes in leading by example. He became a high ranking member of the *gorsedd*[1] at the National Eisteddfod in 2006 in recognition of his services to the Welsh language.

Motivating teachers

Cathy believes: 'The quality of teaching is of paramount importance, as a well-prepared enthusiastic teacher is the key to fostering the feeling that a student is making progress in the language'. Without this inspiration, Cathy doubts whether learners will wish to use Welsh outside class. Cathy's views were endorsed by the other students. Although the main purpose of the qualitative data gathered during the AWLP project was to research learners' experiences outside class, it became clear during the study that, with the exception of Alice, the beginner, all students had had a variety of tutors over the years, some of whom had been far more inspirational than others. Not only knowledge and lesson preparation but also enthusiasm and the ability to create a relaxed atmosphere in the classroom were considered key to both motivating and enabling students to continue learning and using Welsh. Philip felt particularly strongly that a relaxed atmosphere, where students were encouraged and their anxiety was lowered, was of vital importance. As indicated above, he attributes his renewed enthusiasm to attain fluency to the help and inspiration gained on a recent *siop siarad*.

Several students commended one tutor as being particularly good. When asked why this tutor was selected they indicated that she had planned and prepared the lessons well, created a good atmosphere and explained grammar and any important arrangements bilingually. Similarly, in Davies' study of learner integration, respondents considered an enthusiastic tutor a great help not only because they inspired zeal and confidence in their students but because they were usually more ready to provide practical help and to support students' efforts to integrate into the Welsh community (Davies, 2006).

It was interesting that students in the AWLP made the link between teacher motivation and classroom environment as these issues have been given increasing attention in applied linguistics and educational psychology of recent years. Writers such as Dörnyei (2001a) stress the importance of the teacher as a motivator, and identify the teacher's enthusiasm and commitment as among the most important factors in learners' motivation to learn. Dörnyei (2001b: 40–41) also emphasises the value of creating a pleasant and supportive atmosphere in class. What is particularly threatening in the classroom is when: 'Learners are forced to "babble like a child" which might just be the last straw for someone whose personal identity is already unstable or damaged'. He suggests a variety of strategies including the use of humour, encouragement of risk-taking, emphasising that mistakes are a natural part of learning, and stresses the importance of a good physical environment in class.

It was also noteworthy that the first published diary of a Welsh learner (Lewis, 1999: 115, 118–19) stressed the value of an encouraging tutor:

> It seems to me that the teacher has quite a part to play in providing some motivation. Although the urge to learn must come from within, there is no doubt that being congratulated on one's progress is a great support. Learners don't often have the chance to choose their own teachers, but if they do, they should look out for one who is encouraging (...).

As indicated earlier, the onus is ultimately on the learner to overcome obstacles outside class but this is likely to be far easier if the student is content with the help on offer in class. Students inspired by the tutor are more likely to make an effort outside class and Welsh-speakers are thus more likely to take them seriously and support them in their attempts to use Welsh.

Conclusion

It is clear that Welsh learners are quite a heterogeneous group with different motivations for learning. However, the main motivation for the majority is integrative even when the instrumental motive is also present. Whatever motivation the learner has, it is subject to fluctuation, influenced by factors such as anxiety, concerns about their own identities, personal circumstances and stresses related to availability of time for learning and using the language. Some motivators such as learning because a child is in Welsh-medium school or because a significant other is a Welsh-speaker lend themselves to sustained motivation as practice opportunities may take place as part of daily life. However, for many learners such naturalistic practice opportunities do not arise spontaneously and such learners may not be able to sustain motivation when under pressure. Tutors who are second language speakers may be of invaluable help to such learners as they will have been through the system, been subject to various pressures and survived motivation waxing and waning. All tutors however, should be catalysts in inspiring, encouraging and supporting learners to maintain their initial motivation to learn. Ideally, as indicated earlier, the onus should be on the adult learner to move on despite the inevitable plateaux and to return to learning and practising Welsh when circumstances have dictated a period away from the language. However, many learners to date have been unable to do this and have been daunted by the obstacles discussed in Chapters 3 to 6 and ceased learning and using Welsh altogether. In Chapter 8, I will discuss ways in which it may be possible to obviate this diminishing of motivation and enable learners to sustain their initial motivation to gain fluency in Welsh.

Notes

1. Literally means 'throne' in Welsh and is a bardic order which admits those who have made a substantial contribution to Welsh language and culture.

Chapter 8
Conclusions and Recommendations

Introduction

Although the growth in adult Welsh learners over the last 40 years has been remarkable, it remains a matter of great concern to adult educators and language planners that the drop-out rate from WfA classes is high and that relatively few learners progress to become fluent second language speakers.

The main aim of the AWLP was to examine the challenges facing learners when practising Welsh outside the safety of the classroom, using a wide range of methods (interviews, questionnaires, diaries, journals, focus groups, observation, and card sorting activities) as well as drawing on my experiences as a practitioner in WfA and a range of other sources (learners and native speakers; tutors and tutor organisers).

The issues I have discussed in relation to Wales, however, may offer insights for a wide range of other situations. One of the main conclusions of this study is that successful language learners require regular interaction in the target language in a setting in which they feel comfortable, a principle that applies to all L2 learners. Similar issues emerge when learning Chinese in China, English in the United States and German in Germany. The reluctance of native speakers to provide learners with practice where there is a language of wider communication, for example, is a universal theme whether one seeks to use Gaelic in Scotland, Catalan in Catalonia or Javanese in Indonesia.

The Main Findings

As learners struggled to recall their classroom Welsh, they encountered a variety of registers of Welsh, dialect differences, and fluctuating degrees of support from Welsh-speakers who are often perceived as speaking too quickly. One of the main issues that discouraged learners was the tendency of some Welsh-speakers to switch to English, as if doing the learner a favour. Sometimes, identity issues also emerged that disturbed learners, particularly those of Welsh nationality who grew up as monoglot English-speakers.

Learners, of course, have the power to influence the conduct of native speakers. As Larsen-Freeman (2001: 13) has commented: 'A second language learner has a great deal to do with the outcome of the process and is not merely passively dependent on some benevolent, skilful, more proficient interlocutor'. In Chapter 3, I indicated that some AWLP students realised they had the power to influence Welsh-speakers by explaining to them how certain changes in behaviour would help learners gain some much needed practice. Some learners failed to do so and attributed their failure to pressure of circumstances and/or tiredness or because of what they described as laziness. However, although factors such as these may well influence learner behaviour, issues linked with diffidence (see Chapter 5) are likely to play a significant part in the ambivalent reactions of disappointment and relief experienced by so many learners when they miss out on opportunities to use Welsh outside class. Some AWLP learners, nonetheless, developed useful strategies, realising that they could, for instance, ask Welsh-speakers to repeat words and phrases they had not understood; and that they could also make a positive decision to persist in speaking in Welsh even when the Welsh-speaker switched to English. Many learners were also aware that the native speakers suffered from lack of confidence in their own linguistic skills, in particular those whose education had been entirely through English, had lived for long periods outside Wales, or had received limited formal education in either language. This insight helped learners realise that the native speaker's switch to English was not a reflection of the learner's standard of language use and increased their confidence to persist in speaking Welsh.

Bilinguals are unlikely to change their habits to accommodate learners, so it is essential that learners are able to adapt to the native speakers' behaviour. Some, however, lack the courage to do so. Much of their difficulty lies in the fact that learners are straining to understand each word and are easily distracted when dialect is used or the speed of speech increases. This is a situation in which it is easy to apportion blame, but where an understanding of the needs of both groups is helpful. The situation of advanced learners also merits some attention. It is very easy for Welsh-speakers to treat advanced learners as native speakers and to forget, or fail to realise, their limitations. Advanced learners, for their part, may feel more diffident to ask Welsh-speakers to reduce their speed of speech.

Lack of confidence and anxiety emerged as key issues. Many of the learners who participated in the study had 'high affective filters' (Dulay *et al.*, 1982) and would need to find ways forward before 'crossing the bridge' from being L2 learners to L2 speakers. In focus group discussions, AWLP students welcomed the opportunity to discuss their anxieties and their tendencies to shy away from situations that might well help to increase their proficiency. They commented subsequently that they had found the discussion constructive: the realisation that others had experienced similar fears helped to diminish their fears. MacIntyre (2002: 67) notes that an issue as yet unaddressed in the literature, but observed informally among L2 students is: 'the extent to which language anxiety provides a common experience and an opportunity for social exchange. After all, if anxiety leads to misery and misery loves company, then it follows that commiserating about anxiety can be a positive experience, even if the anxiety itself is not'.

Other crucial issues are linked with time and opportunity. There is frequently a disparity between expectations of progress and actual progress: many learners have failed to understand that even conscientious, intelligent adults need to make a substantial investment in practice outside class if fluency is to be achieved. Adult learners have a range of commitments in terms of work, home and family; circumstances sometimes dictate that they are unable to give the time they would wish either to study or to practice. Sometimes, events necessitate that they give up learning for a while until a more settled time in their lives. Many resume learning and may learn intermittently for many years; others give up completely or content themselves with simply 'getting by'.

Opportunity to practice is an issue that troubles many learners who wish to make use of linguistic skills acquired in class in a more naturalistic setting. If students have no Welsh-speaking family, friends, or colleagues, they often find it difficult to practise with acquaintances and in shops. Such learners need to find at least one person with whom they can practise regularly or a domain such as a choir, a sports club, a church, or a public house where they can use the language.

Although instrumental motivation is by no means absent, integrative motivation dominates. Workplace Welsh is problematic to some learners who find it difficult to imagine that they would ever be able to use Welsh in specialised domains. However, there are many success stories in this area. Commitment and support from employers and high motivation from students are essential if Welsh in the workplace is to continue to grow and flourish.

Support for Learners

S. Thomas (2001: 31) is right: 'it's a tough hill to climb alone'. Support is required if learners are to survive potentially damaging experiences on the long road to fluency. It is possible, however, to distinguish between two main kinds of support: the help providers and teachers can offer students in the classroom by way of preparation for using language in the community; and the support native speakers and second language speakers can offer learners.

Support from providers and teachers

As discussed in Chapter 7, good grounding in the classroom and a conscientious, supportive tutor may be sufficient to mobilise many learners to use Welsh outside class. Philip, for instance, disclosed that he had not always felt supported in the community or found classes where he felt comfortable. His attendance at a *siop siarad* where he felt at ease and the new understanding about developing strategies he had gained from writing his dialogue journal, together with the desire to communicate with potential grandchildren, had strengthened his determination; his commitment to attaining fluency was far more powerful. Dissatisfaction with the tutor, classroom methodology, group dynamics or lack of support in the community may well affect commitment; this issue would benefit from further investigations by researchers.

No course on its own, however, can fully prepare most learners for using language in the community (Davies, 2006) for, no matter how hard the teacher tries, the classroom is not the real world. Finding ways of engaging students, in particular the very anxious, so that they feel capable of seizing opportunities to communicate and use their linguistic skills outside class is thus a key issue.

Teachers can offer support of two main kinds: learner preparation which prepares them psychologically for the challenges that face them outside the classroom; and learner strategies which enable learners to cope with the challenges they face in the community. In order to sustain learners' initial motivation and reduce the drop-out rate, it is vital to psychologically prepare learners. Fluency in an L2 as an adult takes time and involves a great deal of work and effort: peaks and troughs in the learning process are accompanied by the waxing and waning of motivation due to pressures both internal and external to the learner. This message needs to be communicated both at the outset and at regular points during the course of study. Tutors who are themselves second language learners often provide credible role models in this task.

As opportunities for naturalistic practice are not always readily available and learners are often ambivalent about seeking them, tutors can instigate a useful boost to speaking skills by making taped speaking with a target language speaker outside class part of the homework. Kluge and Taylor (2000) report that Japanese students of English develop greater fluency if such an activity is made part of the course assessment as the students are thus compelled to make contact with target language speakers who are more likely to be supportive if they view themselves as helping a student gain a qualification. An empathetic tutor, however, is a necessary but not sufficient condition in a learner's success. Neither the maintenance of high standards of teaching nor innovations in methodology are sufficient to obviate issues outside the classroom. Learners also need to be equipped with language learning strategies.

Various writers, including Rubin and Thompson (1982), Wenden (2001), and Oxford (2002), advocate the use of learner preparation and strategies training. Oxford (2002) makes the case that appropriate use of language learning strategies results in improved L2 proficiency overall or in specific language skill areas. Strategies may take very different forms. Cognitive strategies, for instance, entail the effective manipulation of learning materials, including ways of enhancing memory (Chamot, 2001; O'Malley & Chamot, 1990). Metacognitive strategies are useful in the planning, monitoring, and evaluation of language learning activities. For instance, learners may find it helpful to compare their current level of expertise with the course goals on an ongoing basis. Affective strategies serve to control emotions, attitudes and motivation – students may prepare a set of phrases to use with native speakers who speak too quickly for them. Social strategies refer to actions learners take to interact with users of the language, such as searching for opportunities to use the target language. Although cognitive and metacognitive strategies tend to attract more attention in the research, there is evidence that attention to affective and social strategies can be helpful to learners (Oxford *et al.*, 1990; Oxford, 2002).

Rubin (2002), a researcher who has written extensively on the subject of learner strategies, offers independent corroboration for my own observations in comments on entries in the AWLP journals:

> These writers are crying out for strategy training, especially metacognitive training. They need help in defining more realistic goals, not just carrying on a conversation. They need knowledge and practice in using conversational strategies especially those used in holding one's place in a conversation. They need knowledge about affective strategies to overcome their fears and feelings of inadequacy.

How, then, might learner preparation and strategies training be organised? One of the aims of the recent dedicated language centres for adults learning Welsh is to offer students improved support and advice. A possible way forward might be to form a group of experienced professionals in the field of Welsh for adults – providers, tutors and researchers – to evolve a system adapted from the work of researchers in strategy training for the Welsh situation. Any such developments, of course, have obvious funding implications.

Work in this area might be strengthened by – but is not dependent on – centralised support. The findings of the present study can be used by individual tutors to help learners adjust to difficulties encountered in the community in the following ways:

- Advise learners on how to deal with Welsh speakers who turn to English, speak too quickly, and use dialect. They could, for instance, be prepared with useful expressions to use in these situations. Learners who have been forewarned are likely to be more robust in their approach.
- Make learners aware of inconsistencies in a spoken language. As Rubin and Thompson (1982) observe '[real speech] is not simplified, graded or repetitive'. However, the informal environment offers unlimited practice opportunities and can be used initially for listening and later for speaking practice.
- Reassure learners that the Welsh language can be adapted to all domains and point them to online databases of specialised terminology.
- Encourage learners to structure their learning and explain that a high level of time and commitment will be required to ensure success.
- Encourage learners not to be passive but proactive, making the most of all opportunities whether in the target community or when alone by using media, information technology and reading to build on their skills.
- Help learners realise that errors are inevitable and that they cannot progress without taking risks. However, they must be prepared to accept error correction on language issues vital to communication and pronunciation.

Investment in strategy training before and during courses could help decrease the drop-out rate, allowing a higher proportion of learners to progress more quickly to fluency. However, it is vital that strategy training be undertaken in a principled way. Different strategies are appropriate at different levels: for example, while it might be appropriate to introduce dialect forms to intermediate to advanced students to help them in their practice outside class however, it would probably not be wise to use this approach with beginners.

Support from native speakers

There is an urgent need to investigate further the relationship between native speakers and learners and find ways to enable the two groups to work together more productively. Negative attitudes should be eliminated where possible. The following suggestions might be useful:

- Ensure all learners have access to situations or individuals that will help them use Welsh before course completion.
- Extend use of schemes akin to the *CYD Cynllun Pontio*, which pairs native speakers with learners.
- Operate a national friend/mentor system.
- Open drop-in centres for learners/native speakers (this is particularly important in areas like Cardiff, where Welsh is not a community language).
- In the growing use of marketing techniques by the Welsh Language Board, include initiatives that raise the awareness of native speakers to learners' needs.
- Increase media provision specifically for learners.
- Expand the traditional and electronic pen-pal system started by *CYD*.
- Develop training for native speakers committed to language revitalisation to help learners converse with confidence in naturalistic settings. Second language speakers could be particularly useful in this respect, bridging the gap between Welsh learners and Welsh-speakers, though as indicated in Chapter 3, they sometimes need reminding of the needs of learners.
- Study the practice patterns of fluent L2 Welsh-speakers as they may enlighten tutors and learners on how to develop fluency effectively and successfully. Elicit whether they used any specific strategies in order to gain fluency.

The Role of the Adult Welsh Learner in Language Shift

Bobi Jones (1993), the first Welsh learner to hold a university chair in Welsh in Wales, maintains that the revival of Welsh should be based on teaching Welsh to young adults rather than making it compulsory for children, citing the failure of the movement to promote Irish earlier this century where efforts were focused exclusively on the education system. Jones also takes the controversial view that teaching Welsh to children in English-speaking areas is unlikely to succeed because they will have little or no opportunity to use the language when they leave school.

Adults, in contrast, learn of their own volition: they have the power to change the language of a household, influence attitudes and vote. Any attempts to address the problems that cause so many adults to drop out of learning Welsh are therefore likely to make a substantial contribution in the reversal of language shift especially because, as I have indicated in earlier chapters, many of those who do progress to fluency occupy influential positions in many different domains.

There are numerous critics of attempts to reverse language shift in Wales. Christie Davies (1997) expresses the view: 'Welsh people who become fluent in English gain enormously, whereas English people learning Welsh gain very little'. Increased opportunities for children educated through the medium of Welsh when they reach the workplace throw serious doubt on the validity of this observation. Similarly, T. Williams (1997) attributes the increase in learners and second language speakers to an oppressive campaign by an elitist group of native speakers. Given the cognitive, behavioural, and circumstantial barriers that militate against adults learning, however, it is highly unlikely that any adults have crossed the bridge to become Welsh-speakers other than of their own volition. Moreover, adult education is generally an area of second creaming[1], in other words, a high proportion of adult learners already have an educational background; they are likely therefore to form part of the same elite.

It is hoped that the topics discussed in this book will raise issues and strengthen the resolve of tutors, researchers, and learners, not only in Wales, but also in many other situations where the long road to fluency takes the learner outside the classroom and into the community and, in particular, in cases where the target language is in competition with a language of wider communication.

Notes

1. Bengtsson (1975) coined the phrase 'second creaming' in adult education, in other words, those who already have the most education tend to seek adult education programmes rather than those who would benefit from it most. A phenomenon occurs similar to the 'inverse care' law in medicine, where those who need medical care most have least access to it (Hart, 1991). Sargant (2000) reports on a sequence of quantitative surveys of adult participation education in the United Kingdom, which indicates that the gap between the learning rich and learning poor is widening.

Appendix A:
Instructions to Participants for Journal Writing

Private address, phone number and e-mail address supplied at time of research.
E-mail: Lyndapritchard.newcombe@ntlworld.com

Journal Research 16 January – 11 March 2000 – Guidelines for Students

Dear ....

The following are guidelines on the journal research in which you have agreed to participate over the next 8 weeks. If at any time you have any queries please do not hesitate to phone or E-mail me.

* **Purpose**

I would like to understand more about exactly

WHEN, WHERE, HOW and **WITH WHOM** you **SPEAK AND LISTEN TO WELSH OUTSIDE THE CLASSROOM**

Of particular interest is your **reaction** to the conversation
Could you identify any **barriers** or **hindrances**?
Were there any **factors** that particularly **encouraged** you?
Any other relevant comments you may wish to include.

* **Quantity**

I realise that keeping a journal can be time-consuming. For this reason there are no set rules about what or how much you should write. You may write as much or as little as you wish and as often as you wish. There is no need to record every time you use the language, particularly if you speak Welsh frequently most days. However, the more pertinent your comments are the more they will help me understand what can happen when learners attempt to use their skills outside the classroom.

- **Language**

You may write in English, Welsh or a mixture of both.

- **Anonymity**

Only the researchers will know your name. Your names will not be put on the computer records and any reference to you in any published work will be by number or fictitious name.

- **Contact**

I will make brief contact with you by phone or E-mail after you have completed the journal for one month and again two weeks before the end of the project. On completion I would like to spend some time with you discussing your entries at a time and place convenient to you.

- **Meeting for Participants**

I am arranging a meeting for all participants in March or April at my home to discuss some of the points that have arisen about learners' experiences as a result of the journal entries. We will have a snack together as we speak about questions relevant to Welsh learners. This informal gathering will be bilingual and a full translation of all that is said in Welsh will be provided for beginners. I hope you will be able to come as this could be a valuable part of the research project.

Many thanks for your willingness to participate in this project. Your co-operation may well help adult language learners in the future.

References

Abley, M. (2003) *Spoken Here – Travels Among Threatened Languages*. London: Heinemann.

Aitchison, J.W. and Carter, H. (1994) *A Geography of the Welsh Language*. Cardiff: University of Wales Press.

Aitchison, J.W. and Carter, H. (2000) *Language, Economy and Society*. Cardiff: University of Wales Press.

Aitchison, J.W. and Carter, H. (2004) *Spreading the Word*. Talybont: Y Lolfa.

Aldridge, F. (2001) *NIACE Languages Survey*. Leicester: NIACE.

Allen, A.K. (2004) E-mail communication with Lynda Pritchard Newcombe.

Arnold, J. (ed.) (1999) *Affect in Language Learning*. Cambridge: Cambridge University Press.

Arnold, J. and Brown, H.D. (1999) A map of the terrain. In J. Arnold (ed.) *Affect in Language Learning* (pp. 1–24). Cambridge: Cambridge University Press.

Arnold, L. (2004) *Cysgod yn y Coed*. Llandysul: Gomer.

Asher, J.J. (1986) *Learning another Language through Actions*. California, Los Gatos: Sky Oaks Productions.

Bailey, K.M. (1991) Diary studies of classroom language learning: The doubting game and the believing game. In E. Sadtono (ed.) *Language Acquisition & the Second/Foreign Language Classroom* (pp. 60–102). Singapore: Seameo.

Bailey, K.M. and Nunan, D. (eds) (1996) *Voices from the Language Classroom*. Massachusetts: Cambridge: Cambridge University Press.

Baker, C. (1992) *Attitudes & Language*. Clevedon: Multilingual Matters.

Baker, C. (2001) *Foundations of Bilingual Education and Bilingualism* (3rd edn). Clevedon: Multilingual Matters.

Baker, C. and Prys Jones, S. (eds) (1998) *Encyclopedia of Bilingualism and Bilingual Education*. Clevedon: Multilingual Matters.

Ball, M. (ed.) (1993) *The Celtic Languages*. London: Routledge.

Ball, M.A. (1998) Degrees of accentedness in the speech of adult Welsh learners and its effects on the evaluations of Cardiff Welsh-speakers. Unpublished M.A. thesis, Cardiff University, Cardiff.

Ball, M.J. (ed.) (1980) *The Use of Welsh*. Clevedon: Multilingual Matters.

Barnes, J. (1997) Profiad dysgwraig, fforwm iaith Llandrindod, October. Unpublished conference paper.

Barnie, J. (1992) Foreigners. In O. Davies and F. Bowie (eds) *Discovering Welshness* (pp. 118 –121). Llandysul: Gomer.

Bauer, L. and Trudgill, P. (eds) (1998) *Language Myths*. London: Penguin.

Beardsmore, H.B. (ed.) (1993) *European Models of Education*. Clevedon: Multilingual Matters.
Beebe, L. (1983) Risk-taking and the language learner. In H. Seliger and M. Long (eds) *Classroom-oriented Research in Second Language Acquisition* (pp. 39–66). Rowley, Mass: Newbury House.
Bengtsson, J. (1975) Recurrent education and manpower training. *Adult Training* 2, 7–9.
Benson, P. and Nunan, D. (2004) *Learners' Stories*. Cambridge: Cambridge University Press.
Benton, R. and Benton, N. (2001) RLS in Aotearoa/New Zealand 1989–1999. In J. Fishman (ed.) *Can Threatened Languages be Saved?* (pp. 423–450). Clevedon: Multilingual Matters.
Betts, C. (2001) Only Welsh-speakers are truly Welsh. *Western Mail*, 21 October, 1.
Beynon, J.H. (2006) Interview with Lynda Pritchard Newcombe.
Bianchi, T. (1992) The Last Laugh. In O. Davies and F. Bowie (eds) *Discovering Welshness* (pp. 164–171). Llandysul: Gomer.
Black, R., Gillies, W. and Ó Maolalaigh, R. (eds) (1999) *Celtic Connections, Proceedings of the Tenth International Congress of Celtic Studies*. East Lothian: Tuckwell Press.
Boak, P. (2005) E-mail communication with Lynda Pritchard Newcombe.
Bohren, C.F. (1978) Y dysgwr. *Y Faner*. September, 1.
Bohren, C.F. (2006) E-mail communication with Lynda Pritchard Newcombe.
Bowie, F. (1993) Wales from within: Conflicting interpretations of Welsh identity. In S. MacDonald (ed.) *Inside European Identities* (pp. 167–193). Oxford: Berg.
Breen, M. (ed.) (2001) *Learner Contributions to Language Learning: New Directions in Research*. Harlow: Pearson Education.
British Council (2005) Welsh Language Project Annual Report. On WWW at http://www.britishcouncil.org/wales-education-welsh-language-project.htm.
Brown, H.D. (2000) *Principles of Language Teaching*. White Plains, NY: Longman.
Brown, J.P. (1971) Welcoming the Welsh learner. *Planet* 7, 39–41.
Brumfit, C.J. and Roberts, T.J. (1983) *Language and Language Teaching*. London: Batsford.
Burdett-Jones, M. (2002) Interview with Lynda Pritchard Newcombe.
Burdett-Jones, M. (2004) Interview with Lynda Pritchard Newcombe.
Burt, M., Dulay, H. and Finocchiaro, M. (eds) (1977) *Viewpoints on English as a Second Language*. New York: Regents.
Camardons, J.S., Castaño, J. and Diaz, A. (2005) *Volunteers for Language*. Linguistic Integration Programme in Catalan: Facts for Evaluation, Noves SL, Revista de Sociolinguistica. On WWW at http://www.gencat.net/ptrifrnvis/Nengcat/noves.
Castle, C. (2002) E-mail communication with Lynda Pritchard Newcombe.
Chamot, A. (2001) The role of learner strategies in second language acquisition. In M. Breen (ed.) *Learner Contributions to Language Learning: New Directions in Research* (pp. 25–43). Harlow: Pearson Education.
Childs, M. (2004) Welsh experiences of bilingualism. *Daily Yomiuri*. 13 August, 14.
Church, B. (2002) *Learn Greek in 25 Years – A Crash Course for the Linguistically Challenged*. Athens Athens: News.
Cilt (2005) *Language Trends 2005 – Adult Language Learning in England*. On WWW at http://www.cilt.org.uk/key/trends2005/trends2005_adults.pdf.

Clark, R. (2005) Move brings brighter future for London Welsh School. *Western Mail*, 2 June, 26.

Clayton, P. (1996) *Gofal Dysgwyr.* Llanrwst: Gwasg Carreg Gwalch.

Clément, R. and Gardner, R. (2001) Second language mastery. In W.P. Robinson and H. Giles (eds) *The New Handbook of Language and Social Psychology* (pp. 489–504). Chichester: Wiley & Sons.

Clowes, C. (1992) Modd i fyw. In O. Davies and F. Bowie (eds) *Discovering Welshness* (pp. 59–69). Llandysul: Gomer.

Cohen, A.D. (1998) *Strategies in Learning and Using a Second Language.* London: Longman.

Cole, S. (1998) *A Passionate Life.* London: Hodder & Stoughton.

Comings, J., Parrella, A. and Soricone, L. (2000) *Helping Adults Persist: Four Supports.* On WWW at http://gseweb.harvard.edu/~ncsall/fob/2000/comings.html.

Comunn Na Gaidhlig (1992) *Feumalachdan Luchd-Ionnsachaidh, Rannsachadh Nàiseanta* [Provision for Gaelic Learners, National Survey]. Inverness Comunn Na Gaidhlig.

Comunn Na Gaidhlig (1994) *Comann an Luchd-Ionnsachaidh.* [The Voice of Gaelic Learners]. December, Inverness: Comunn Na Gaidhig.

Conlon, E. and Davies, E. (2006) *Cwrs Canolradd.* Cardiff: WJEC.

Cook, V. (2002) (ed.) *Portraits of the L2 User.* Clevedon: Multilingual Matters.

Cope, C. (2006) Learning Welsh through the Internet. Unpublished paper given on 10th August, 2006 in Maes D, National Eisteddfod, Swansea.

Corder, S.P. (1981) *Error Analysis and Interlanguage.* Oxford: Oxford University Press.

Coupland, N. (ed.) (1990) *English in Wales.* Clevedon: Multilingual Matters.

Crookes, G. and Schmidt, R. (1991) Language learning motivation: Reopening the research agenda. *Language Learning* 41, 469–512.

Crystal, D. (2000) *Language Death.* Cambridge: Cambridge University Press.

Curran, C.A. (1972) *Counseling-Learning: A Whole-Person Model for Education.* New York: Grune & Stratton.

Dafis, Ll. (1985) Bwrw Swildod. *Y Faner*, 17 July, 14–15.

Dalby, A. (2002) *Language in Danger.* London: Allen Lane.

Daugherty, R., Phillips, R. and Rees, G. (eds) (2000) *Education Policy-Making in Wales–Explorations in Devolved Governance.* Cardiff: University of Wales Press.

Davidson, I. and Piette, B. (2000) Without & Within: Inclusion, identity and continuing education in a new Wales. University of Wales, Bangor. Paper presented at SCUTREA 30th Annual Conference, 3–5 July 2000, University of Nottingham. On WWW at www.leeds.ac.uk/educol/documents/00001441.htm.

Davies, B. (1995) Interview with Lynda Pritchard Newcombe.

Davies, Cennard (1973) *Dros y Bont.* Llandysul: Gomer.

Davies, Cennard (1978) When you first start to speak: Some learners' problems. In P. Finch (ed.) *How to Learn Welsh* (pp. 39–53). Swansea: Christopher Davies.

Davies, Cennard (1980) Living Welsh. In M.J. Ball (ed.) *The Use of Welsh* (pp. 200–210). Clevedon: Multilingual Matters.

Davies, Cennard (2000) Y dosbarth a'r gymdeithas. In C. Jones (ed.) *Cyflwyno'r Gymraeg* (pp. 160–172). Llandysul: Gomer.

Davies, Cennard (2001) Interview with Lynda Pritchard Newcombe.

Davies, Christie (1997) Minority language and social division. In G. Frost (ed.) *Loyalty Misplaced* (pp. 39–47). Reading: The Social Affairs Unit.

Davies, D. (2005a) Spread Welsh – persuade the children to use it. *Western Mail,* 1 June, 12.

Davies, D. (2005b) Cardiff mum is fifth woman to win Eisteddfod crown. *Western Mail,* 2 August, 14.

Davies, Elaine (2005) Welsh in the family. *Agenda,* Summer issue, 12.

Davies, Emyr (2000) Dulliau dysgu a'r dosbarth iaith. In C. Jones (ed.) *Cyflwyno'r Gymraeg* (pp. 11–26). Llandysul: Gomer.

Davies, Emyr (2005) Developing resources for language tutors – ensuring positive washback. Paper given at the ALTE Conference in Cardiff on 11 November, 2005.

Davies, Janet (1993) *The Welsh Language.* Cardiff: University of Wales Press.

Davies, Janet (1999) *A Pocket Guide – The Welsh Language.* Cardiff: University of Wales Press.

Davies, John (1993) *A History of Wales.* Penguin Books: London.

Davies, J.P. (1986) Dadansoddiad o Nodau Graddedig ar gyfer Oedolion sydd yn dysgu Cymraeg. Unpublished Ph.D., University of Wales, Bangor.

Davies, L. (2006) Integrating Welsh learners into the Welsh community and its implications for the Welsh tutor. Unpublished assignment submitted in part fulfillment of Post Graduate Certificate in Education Post-Compulsory Education and Training, Cardiff University.

Davies, O. (1992) Welsh hills. In O. Davies and F. Bowie (eds) *Discovering Welshness* (pp. 74–76). Llandysul: Gomer.

Davies, O. and Bowie, F. (1992) (eds.) *Discovering Welshness.* Llandysul: Gomer.

Davies, P. (1992) A disservice to Welsh scholarship. In O. Davies and F. Bowie (eds) *Discovering Welshness* (pp. 40–43). Llandysul: Gomer.

Deuchar, M. (2006) Welsh-English code-switching and the Matrix Language frame model. *Lingua* 116 (11), 1986–2011.

Devine, D. (2005) Watch with mother! Welsh from Sali Mali. *Western Mail,* 17 February, 34–35.

Dodson, C.J. (1967) *Language Teaching and the Bilingual Method.* London: Pitman.

Dörnyei, Z. (1998) Motivation in second and foreign language learning. *Language Teaching* 31, 117–35.

Dörnyei, Z. (2001a) *Teaching and Researching Motivation.* Harlow: Longman.

Dörnyei, Z. (2001b) *Motivational Strategies in the Language Classroom.* Cambridge: Cambridge University Press.

Dufon, M. (1999) E-mail communication with Lynda Pritchard Newcombe.

Duggan, M.A.K. (1992) Adnabod, Hanfod, Cymreictod. In O. Davies and F. Bowie (eds) *Discovering Welshness* (pp. 136–147). Llandysul: Gomer.

Dulay, H., Krashen, S.D. and Burt, M. (1982) *Language two.* Oxford: Oxford University Press.

Duncan, A. (1998) 'The funny thing is I love life'. *Radio Times,* 18–24 April, 13–14.

Dyfed, E. (1979) Tudalen y dysgwyr. *Barn,* 203/4, 269–70.

Edwards, V.K. and Newcombe, L.P. (2003) *Evaluation of the Efficiency and Effectiveness of the Twf Project, Which Encourages Parents to Transmit the Language to their Children.* Cardiff: Welsh Language Board.

Edwards, V.K. and Newcombe, L.P. (2005a) When school is not enough: New initiatives in intergenerational language transmission in Wales. *International Journal of Bilingualism and Bilingual Education* 8(4), 298–312.

Edwards, V.K. and Newcombe, L.P. (2005b) Language transmission in the family in Wales: An example of innovative language planning. *Language Planning and Language Problems* 29(2), 135–150.

Ehrman, M.E. (1996) *Understanding Second Language Learning Difficulties*. Thousand Oaks, California: Sage.

Elliot, J., *et al.* (eds) (1996) *Communities and their Universities*. London: Lawrence & Wishart.

ELWa (2005) *All You Need to Know About Learning Welsh (but were too afraid to ask)*. Cardiff: ELWa.

Enfield, E. (2003) *Greece on My Wheels*. Essex: Summersdale.

Estyn (2004) *The Quality of Provision in Welsh for Adults*. Estyn, Cardiff: Her Majesty's Inspectorate of Education and Training in Wales.

Evans, A. (2004) Unpublished autobiography of language learning.

Evans, G. (1969) Digwyddodd yn Israel. *Barn* 78, 152–153.

Evans, G. (2000) Cymru 2000. *Cambria* 3(4), 14–15.

Evans, L. (1989) 'Tyllau Bwtwn'. In M. Rhys (ed.) *Ar Fy Myw* (pp. 15–22). Dinas Powys: Honno.

Evas, J. (1999) Rhwystrau ar Lwybr Dwyiethrwydd. Unpublished Ph.D. thesis, Cardiff University.

Evas, J. (2001) Dulliau dysgu awgrym er gwell. *Cylchgrawn Addysg Cymru*. Vol. 10(1), 32–45.

Fehlen, F. (1997) Pre-eminent role of linguist capital in the reproduction of the social space in Luxembourg. In M. Grenfell and M. Kelly (eds) *Bourdieu. Culture & Education* (pp. 61–72). New York: Peter Lang.

Ferguson, C.A. (1959) Diglossia. *Word* 15(2), 325–40.

Finch P. (ed.) (1978) *How to Learn Welsh*. Swansea: Christopher Davies.

Fenton, R. (2002) E-mail communication with Lynda Pritchard Newcombe.

First Peoples' Cultural Foundation (2003) On WWW at http://www.fpcf.ca/lang-firstvoices.html.

Firth, A. and Wagner, J. (1998) SLA–No trespassing. *Modern Language Journal* 82, 91–4.

Fishman, J. (1967) Bilingualism with and without diglossia; diglossia with and without bilingualism. In J. MacNamara (ed.) Problems of Bilingualism. *Journal of Social Issues* 23: 29–38.

Fishman, J. (1991) *Reversing Language Shift*. Clevedon: Multilingual Matters.

Fishman, J. (ed.) (2001) *Can Threatened Languages be Saved?* Clevedon: Multilingual Matters.

Frost, G. (ed.) (1997) *Loyalty Misplaced*. Reading: The Social Affairs Unit.

Gardner, R.C. (1985) *Social Psychology and Second Language Learning*. London: Arnold.

Gardner, R.C. (2001) *Integrative Motivation: Past, Present and Future*. On WWW at http://publish/uwo.ca/~gardner/GardnerPublicLecture1.pdf.

Gardner, R.C. and Lambert, W. (1959) Motivational variables in second language acquisition. *Canadian Journal of Psychology* 13, 266–272.

Gardner, R.C. and Lambert, W. (1972) *Attitudes and Motivation in Second Language Learning*. Rowley, Massachusetts: Newbury House.

Gardner, R.C. and MacIntyre, P.D. (1991) An instrumental motivation in language study: Who says it isn't effective? *Studies in Second Language Acquisition* 13, 57–72.

Gardner, R.C. and Tremblay, P.E. (1994) On motivation, measurement and conceptual considerations. *Modern Language Journal* 78, 524–527.

Garlick, E. (1968) Adfywiad yr Hebraeg. *Barn* 71, 296–297.

Gattegno, C. (1972) *Teaching Foreign Languages in Schools – the Silent Way*. New York: Educational Solutions.
Gillibrand, J. (1992) A language to live by. In O. Davies and F. Bowie (eds) *Discovering Welshness* (pp. 31–34). Llandysul: Gomer.
Glyn, S. (2002) E-mail communication with Lynda Pritchard Newcombe.
Greenslade, D. (1992) *Burning Down the Dosbarth*. Talybont: Y Lolfa.
Greenwood, K. (1971) Gair am Saesnes Druenes. *Barn* 124, 164–165.
Grenfell, M. and Kelly, M. (eds) (1999) *Bourdieu. Culture & Education*. New York: Peter Lang.
Griffiths, G. (2001) Yr Iaith ar Daith ar y Bws yn y Cymoedd. *Y Cymro*, 21 July, 8.
Griffiths, M. (ed.) (1997) *The Welsh Language in Education* (pp. 95–98). Cardiff: WJEC.
Gruffudd, H. (1979) Tudalen y dysgwyr. *Barn* 200, 131–132.
Gruffudd, H. (1980) Tudalen y dysgwyr. *Barn* 205, 13.
Gruffudd, H. (2000) Planning for the use of Welsh by young people. In C.H. Williams (ed.) *Language Revitalisation* (pp. 173–207). Cardiff: University of Wales Press.
Guus, E. and Gorter, D. (eds.) (2001) *The Other Languages of Europe*. Clevedon: Multilingual Matters.
Gwynedd, M. (1999) Yma o hyd – Nant Gwrtheyrn. *Lingo Newydd*. March/April, 12.
Hampâté Ba, A. (1996) Oui, mon commandant. *Mémoires* (vol. 2). Paris: Actes Sud.
Harlow, R. (1998) Some languages are just not good enough. In L. Bauer and P. Trudgill (eds) *Language Myths* (pp. 10–14). London: Penguin.
Harris, J. (2001) Dysgu Cymraeg. *Y Wawr* 133, 18.
Hart, J.T. (1991) The inverse care law. In P. Worsley *The New Modern Sociology Readings* (pp. 264–265). London: Penguin.
Hawkins, E. (1996) Language teaching in perspective. In E. Hawkins (ed.) *30 Years of Language Teaching* (pp. 15–32). London: CILT.
Hawkins, E. (ed.) (1996) *30 Years of Language Teaching*. London: CILT.
Hedges, K. (2005) A candidate's perspective. Paper given at the ALTE Conference in Cardiff on 11 November, 2005.
Higham, M. (2002) Unpublished autobiography of language learning.
Hill, G. (1987) English voices. *Planet* 64, 14–19.
Her Majesty's Inspectors' (HMI) Report 12 (1984) *Teaching Welsh as a Second Language to Adults*. Cardiff: The Welsh Office.
Hooper, W. (ed) (1966) *Of Other Worlds: Essays & Stories*. London: Geoffrey Bles.
Horwitz, E. (2001) Language anxiety and achievement. *Annual Review of Applied Linguistics* 21, 112–126.
Hughes, E. (2002) Interview with Lynda Pritchard Newcombe.
Hughes, E. (2005) The social context for adults learning Welsh. Paper at the ALTE Conference in Cardiff on 11 November, 2005.
Hughes, E.J. (ed.) (2005) *Geiriadur Deintyddiaeth*. Llandybïe: Gwasg Dinefwr.
Hughes, H. (2003) Cymathu'r Dysgwyr â'r Gymdeithas Gymraeg a rôl yr addysgwyr yn y broses. Unpublished M.A. thesis, Cardiff University.
Hughes, H. (2006) E-mail communication with Lynda Pritchard Newcombe.
Hughes, M. (1989) *Selecting, Adapting and Creating Communicative Material for Welsh Learners*. The Language Unit, The North East Wales Institute of Higher Education.
Hume, I. and Pryce, W.T.R. (1986) *The Welsh and Their Country*. Llandysul: Gomer.
Hunter, H. (2006) *Dyfal Donc*. Talybont, Ceredigion: Y Lolfa.

Hymes, D. (1972) On communicative competence. In J. Pride and J. Holmes (eds) *Sociolinguistics* (pp. 289–293). London: Penguin.

Jacobs, N. (1976) Learning Welsh 3. *Planet* 34, 14–15.

James, D.L. (1971) Seiliau dysgu Ail Iaith. *Yr Athro* 22(8), 223–227.

James, D.L. (1974a) Ulpan Gymraeg Aberystwyth (1), *Yr Athro* 26(4), 106–116.

James, D.L. (1974b) Cymraeg Eisteddfod. *Yr Athro* 25(5), 143–147.

James, M. (1998) Troi'r dysgwyr yn Gymry. *Y Faner Newydd* 9, 7.

James-Traille, A. (2002) Telephone interview with Lynda Pritchard Newcombe.

Jenkins, G. (ed.) (1999) *Llyfr y Ganrif*. Aberystwyth: Llyfrgell Genedlaethol Cymru a'r Lolfa.

Jenkins, G.H. (ed.) (2000a) *The Welsh Language and its Social Domains 1901–1911*. Cardiff: University of Wales Press.

Jenkins, G.H. (2000b) Terminal decline? The Welsh language in the twentieth century. Keynote address at the 2000 Conference North American Association for the Study of Welsh Culture and History at Brynmawr College, Pennsylvania.

Jenkins, G.H. and Williams, M. (2000) The fortunes of the Welsh language 1900–2000: Introduction. In G.H. Jenkins and M. Williams (eds) *'Let's Do Our Best for the Ancient Tongue' The Welsh Language in the Twentieth Century* (pp. 1–27). Cardiff: University of Wales Press.

Jenkins, G.H. and Williams, M. (eds) (2000) *'Let's Do Our Best for the Ancient Tongue' The Welsh Language in the Twentieth Century*. Cardiff: University of Wales Press.

Johnstone, D. (2006) What lessons can we all learn from developments in minority and regional language education in particular in pre-school and school education? Plenary address at Regional and Minority Languages in Education Systems Conference. Brussels, 28 April.

Jones, A. (2003) On WWW at http://www.bbc.co.uk/wales/mid/sites/eisteddfod_2003/pages/aran_jones.shtml.

Jones, A. and Jones, B. (2001) *Welsh Reflection: Y Drych & America 1851–2001*. Llandysul: Gomer.

Jones, B. (1993) *Language Regained*. Llandysul: Gomer.

Jones, C. (1991) The Ulpan in Wales: A study in motivation. *Journal of Multilingual and Multicultural Development* 12(3), 183–193.

Jones, C. (ed.) (2000) *Cyflwyno'r Gymraeg*. Llandysul: Gomer.

Jones, E. (ed.) (2000) *The Welsh in London 1500–2000*. Cardiff: University of Wales Press.

Jones, G.W. (1993) *Agweddau ar Ddysgu Iaith*. Llandysul: Gomer.

Jones, K. (2000) 'Siarad Cymraeg pob cyfle': How and why in-migrant Welsh learners use Welsh the way they do. In P.W. Thomas and J. Mathias (eds) *Developing Minority Languages* (pp. 639–651). Department of Welsh, Cardiff University, with Llandysul: Gomer.

Jones, N. (1989) Blod and the brush Salesman. *Planet* 76, 9–13.

Jones, N. (1992) 'Rhiannon, Mabon & Me'. In O. Davies and F. Bowie (eds) *Discovering Welshness* (pp. 121–127). Llandysul: Gomer.

Jones, N. (1993) *Living in Rural Wales*. Llandysul: Gomer.

Jones, O.G. (1962) *Llyfryddiaeth Dysgu Cymraeg fel Ail-iaith*. Aberystwyth: Cyfadran Addysg Coleg Prifysgol Cymru.

Jones, R. (2005) *Bilingual Nation? Consumer Attitudes to Learning Welsh*. Welsh Consumer Council.

Jones, R. (2006) Croeso a dawns yn Rhuthun, *Y Wawr* 151, 20.

Jones, R.M. (1962) Theori dysgu ail iaith. *Yr Athro* 13(1), 14–18.

Jones, R.M. (1974) The roots of Welsh inferiority. *Planet* 22, 53–72.

Jones, R.O. (1993) The sociolinguistics of Welsh. In M. Ball (ed.) *The Celtic Languages* (pp. 536–605). London: Routledge.

Jones, R.O. (1999) The Welsh language. In R. Black, W. Gillies and R. Ó Maolalaigh (eds) *Celtic Connections, Proceedings of the Tenth International Congress of Celtic Studies* (pp. 425–456). East Lothian: Tuckwell Press.

Jones, R.O. (2001) *Cynllun yr Iaith Gymraeg yn Chubut, Adroddiad Arolwg 2001*. Canolfan Dysgu Cymraeg, Adran y Gymraeg, Prifysgol, Caerdydd.

Jones, R.O. (2002) Interview with Lynda Pritchard Newcombe.

Jones, R.O. and Newcombe, L.P. (2002) *Llyfryddiaeth dysgu'r Gymraeg yn ail iaith i oedolion 1960–2002: heb ei gyhoeddi*. Caerdydd: Bwrdd yr Iaith. (Unpublished bibliography for the Welsh Language Board). On WWW at http://www.bwrdd-yr-iaith.org.uk/cy/cynnwys.php?cID=6&pID=109&nID =166.

Jones, R.O. (2006) Dysgwyr ym Mhatagonia. Unpublished paper given on 10th August, 2006 in Maes D, National Eisteddfod, Swansea.

Jones-Williams, M. (2002) Chwys a chwerthin dros yr iaith. *Western Mail Magazine* 16 February, 18–19.

Khleif, B. (1978) Ethnic awakening in the 1st world: The case of Wales. In G. Williams (ed.) *Social and Cultural Change in Contemporary Wales* (pp. 102–109). London: Routledge.

Kiff, G. (2001) *Adroddiad Blynyddol y Swyddog Datblygu 2000–2001*. Caerdydd: Bwrdd yr Iaith Gymraeg.

Kinney, P. (1992) A hidden culture. In O. Davies and F. Bowie (eds) *Discovering Welshness* (pp. 1–5). Llandysul: Gomer.

Kluge, D. and Taylor, M.A. (2000) *Boosting Speaking Fluency through Partner Taping.* On WWW at http://iteslj.org/Techniques/Kluge-PartnerTaping.html.

Knowles, M. (1978) *The Adult Learner: A Neglected Species* (2nd edn). Houston: Gulf Publishing.

Kodesh, S. (1982) *Hebrew as a Spoken Language.* Jerusalem: Tarbuth Foundation, Ktav Publishing House.

Krashen, S.D. (1977) The monitor model for second language performance. In M. Burt, H. Dulay and M. Finocchiaro (eds) *Viewpoints on English as a Second Language* (pp. 152–161). New York: Regents.

Krashen, S. and Terrell, T.D. (1983) *The Natural Approach; Language Acquisition in the Classroom.* Oxford: Pergamon Press.

Krashner, H. and Taylor, J. (1992) Profiad dwy sy wedi symud i ochr arall y bwrdd. *Y Tiwtor,* Spring, 18.

Lamping, A. and Ball, C. (1996) *Maintaining Motivation.* London: CILT.

Larsen-Freeman, D. and Long, M. (1991) *An Introduction to Second Language Acquisition Research.* London: Longman.

Larsen-Freeman, D. (2001) Individual cognitive/affective learner contributions and differential success in second language acquisition. In M. Breen (ed.) *Learner Contributions to Language Learning: New Directions in Research* (pp. 12–24). Harlow: Pearson Education.

Layland, A. (2001) Interview with Lynda Pritchard Newcombe.

Layland, A. (2004) E-mail communication with Lynda Pritchard Newcombe.

Lewis, C.S. (1966) On three ways of writing for children. In W. Hooper (ed.) *Of Other Worlds: Essays & Stories.* London: Geoffrey Bles.

Lewis, D.H. (2001) Learning Welsh and learning Welshness: An insider's view from performance to participation. Unpublished BA Project, Lampeter, University College of Wales.

Lewis, G. (1998) Review – Travels in an old tongue, *Planet* 127, 99–101.

Lewis, M. (1999) *How to Study Foreign Languages.* Basingstoke: Macmillan.

Lewis, M. (2003) Interview with Lynda Pritchard Newcombe.

Lewis, R. (1969) *Second-Class Citizen.* Llandysul: Gomer.

Lewis, R. (1992) *Geiriadur y Gyfraith.* Llandysul: Gomer.

Liu, M. (2006) Anxiety in Chinese EFL students at different proficiency levels. *System* 34(3), 301–316.

Liu, Z. (1984) *Two Years in the Melting Pot.* San Francisco: China Books and Periodicals.

Loveday, L. (1982) *The Sociolinguistics of Learning and Using a Non-Native Language.* Oxford: Pergamon Press.

Lozanov, G. (1979) *Suggestology and Outlines of Suggestopedy.* New York: Gordon & Breach Science Publishers.

Lvovich, N. (1997) *The Multilingual Self – An Inquiry into Language Learning.* Mahwah, New Jersey: Lawrence Erlbaum.

MacCaluim, A. (2000) On the periphery of the periphery – Gaelic learners in the revival of Gaelic. Paper delivered to the Gaelic Society of Perth, 11 November.

MacDonald, S. (ed.) (1993) *Inside European Identities.* Oxford: Berg.

MacIntyre, P.D. (1995) How does anxiety affect second language? – A reply to Sparks & Ganshow. *Modern Language Journal* 79(i), 90–99.

MacIntyre, P.D. (2002) Motivation, anxiety and emotion in second language acquisition. In P. Robinson *Individual Difference and Instructed Language Learning* (pp. 45–68). Amsterdam: John Benjamins.

MacIntyre, P.D., Clément, R. and Conrod, S. (2001) Willingness to communicate, social support and language-learning orientations of immersion students. *Studies in Second Language Acquisition* 23(3), 369–388.

MacIntyre, P.D. and Gardner, R.C. (1989) Anxiety and second language learning: Toward a theoretical clarification. *Language Learning* 39(2), 251–275.

MacIntyre, P.D. and Gardner, R.C. (1991) Methods and results in the study of anxiety and language learning: A review of the literature. *Language Learning* 41(1), 85–117.

MacIntyre, P.D., Noels, K.A. and Clément, R. (1997) Biases in self-ratings of second language proficiency: The role of language anxiety. *Language Learning* 47(2), 265–287.

MacNamara, J. (ed.) (1967) Problems of bilingualism. *Journal of Social Issues* 23, 29–38.

Macri, M. (2004) *Native American Studies.* On WWW at http://nas.ucdavis.edu/.

Maro, J. (1971) Adferiad Israel. *Taliesin* 23, 96–111.

Marsden, P. (2001) E-mail communication with Lynda Pritchard Newcombe.

Martin-Short, L. (1998) Profiad yn Dysgu Cymraeg. *Y Wawr* 120, 19.

May, S. (2000) Accommodating and resisting minority language policy: The case of Wales. *International Journal of Bilingual Education and Bilingualism* 3(2), 101–128.

McCaughey, P.E. (2001/2) Cymdeithas Madog presents: Y Cwrs ar y paith – The course on the prairie. *Y Drych* 151(1), 7.

McCoy, G. and Maolcholaim, S. (2000) (eds) *Aithre na Ngael*. Queen's University, Belfast: Institute of Irish Studies.

Meek, E. (2005) *Cwrs Mynediad*. Cardiff: WJEC.

Morgan, L. (2002) Telephone interview with Lynda Pritchard Newcombe.

Morgan, P. (2000) The Gael is dead: Long live the Gael: The changing relationship between native and learner Gaelic users. In G. McCoy and S. Maolcholaim (eds) *Aithre na Ngael* (pp. 126–132). Queen's University, Belfast: Institute of Irish Studies.

Morgan, W.J. (1955) A Capital City. *The Observer*, 25 December, 5.

Morris, S. (1993) Dysgwyr a Thafodieithoedd. *Barn* 368, 9–10.

Morris, S. (1996) The Welsh language and its restoration. In J. Elliot *et al.* (eds) *Communities and their Universities* (pp. 148–163). London: Lawrence & Wishart.

Morris, S. (1997) Language minorities and minority languages in the changing Europe. In *Proceedings of the 6th International Conference on Minority Languages, Gdansk, 1–5 July 1996*. Gdansk Wydawnictwo Uniwersytetu Gdanskiego, Gdansk.

Morris, S. (2000a) Welsh adults: A policy for a bilingual Wales? In R. Daugherty, R. Phillips and G. Rees (eds) *Education Policy-Making in Wales–Explorations in Devolved Governance* (pp. 239–235). Cardiff: University of Wales Press.

Morris, S. (2000b) Adult education, language revival and language planning. In C.H. Williams (ed.) *Language Revitalisation* (pp. 208–220). Cardiff: University of Wales Press.

Morris, S. (2001) Language planning strategies for integrating adult learners: Crossing the bridge between Yish and Xish. Paper from 2nd European Conference on Language Planning on 14 November at Andorra La Vella.

Naiman, N. *et al.* (1996) *The Good Language Learner*. Clevedon: Multilingual Matters.

Newcombe, L. (1995) An evaluation of the WLPAN method of learning Welsh at the Welsh language teaching centre, University of Wales College of Cardiff. Unpublished M.Ed. Thesis, Cardiff University.

Newcombe, L.P. (2001) *The English Not: Practising German*. Unpublished diary.

Newcombe, L.P. and Newcombe, R.G. (2001a) Adult language learning: The effect of background, motivation and practice on perseverance. *International Journal of Bilingual Education and Bilingualism* 4(5), 332–354.

Newcombe, L.P. and Newcombe, R.G. (2001b) "The 'bwlch' is great"–Welsh learners' voices. *Welsh Journal of Education* 10(2), 72–91.

Newcombe, L.P. (2002a) Snakes and ladders. *Planet* 151, 86–92.

Newcombe, L.P. (2002b) "A tough hill to climb alone"–Welsh learners speak. *Hong Kong Journal of Applied Linguistics* 7(2), 39–56.

Newcombe, L.P. (2002c) The relevance of social context in the education of adult Welsh learners. Unpublished Ph.D. thesis, Cardiff University.

Newcombe, L.P. (2004) Adroddiad Gwerthuso effeithlonrwydd *CYD* – mudiad sy'n dod â Dysgwyr a Chymry Cymraeg at ei gilydd yn gymdeithasol. *CYD*, Aberystwyth. (Unpublished report for *CYD*).

Newcombe, R.G. and Soto, C.M. (2006) Intervalos de Confianza para las Estimaciones de Proporciones y las Diferencias Entre Ellas. *Interdisciplinaria – Revista de Psicologia y Ciencias Afines* 23(2), 141–154.

Norton, B. (1998) Using journals in second language research and teaching. In T. Smoke (ed.) *Pedagogy & Participation in Classroom and Community Contexts* (pp. 55–71). Mahwah, New Jersey: Erlbaum.

Norton, B. and Toohey, K. (2001) Changing perspectives on good language learners. *TESOL Quarterly* 35(2), 307–322.

Nunan, D. (1989) *Understanding Language Classrooms.* New York: Prentice-Hall.

O'Malley, J.M. and Chamot, A.U. (1990) *Learning Strategies in Second Language Acquisition.* Cambridge: Cambridge University Press.

O'Neill, D. (2005) *Rebuilding the Celtic Languages.* Talybont, Ceredigion: Y Lolfa.

Osmond, J. (1973) ULPAN experiment may point way to fluency in Welsh. *Western Mail,* 7 December, 11.

Oxford, R.L. (1990) *Language Learning Strategies – What Every Teacher Should Know.* New York: Newbury House.

Oxford, R.L., Crookall, D., Cohen, A.D., Lawine, R.Z., Nyikos, M. and Sutter, W. (1990) Strategy training for language learners: Six situational case studies and a training model. *Foreign Language Annals* 22, 197–216.

Oxford, R.L. and Shearin, J. (1994) Language learning motivation: Expanding the theoretical framework, *The Modern Language Journal* 78(1), 12–28.

Oxford, R.L. (1999) Anxiety and the language learner: New insights. In J. Arnold (ed.) *Affect in Language Learning* (pp. 58–67). Cambridge: Cambridge University Press.

Oxford, R.L. (2002) Language learning strategies in a nutshell: Update and ESL suggestions. In J.C. Richards and W.A. Renandya (eds) *Methodology in Language Teaching* (pp. 124–132). Cambridge: Cambridge University Press.

Pegrum, M.A. (2000) The outside world as an extension of the EFL/ESL classroom. *The Internet TESL Journal* 7(7). On WWW at http://iteslj.org/.

Perales, J. (2003) E-mail to Haydn Hughes, 11 February, 2003.

Perryman, J. (2004) Unpublished autobiography of language learning.

Petro, P. (1997) *Travels in an Old Tongue.* London: Harper Collins.

Petro, P. (2002) E-mail communication with Lynda Pritchard Newcombe.

Peyton, J.K. and Reed, L. (1990) *Dialogue Journal Writing with Non-Native Speakers.* Virginia: TESOL.

Pfeiffer, N. (2004) Unpublished autobiography of language learning.

Pierce, B.N. (1993) Language learning, social identity and immigrant women. Unpublished Ph.D., Ontario Institute for Studies in Education, University of Toronto.

Pierce, B.N. (1995) Social identity, investment, and language learning. *TESOL Quarterly* 29(1), 9–31.

Polani, H. (1978) Letter from Ministry of Education and Culture, Jerusalem to Councillor J.R.P. Evans, Gwent.

Preston, J. (1997) Unpublished autobiography of language learning.

Price, A. (2001) Interview with Lynda Pritchard Newcombe.

Price, G. (1985) *The Languages of Britain.* London: Arnold.

Pride, J. and Holmes, J. (eds) (1972) *Sociolinguistics.* London: Penguin.

Prosser, H. (1985) *Llyfryddiaeth dysgu'r Gymraeg yn ail iaith: 1961–1981.* Aberystwyth: Canolfan Ymchwil Cymraeg i Oedolion, Coleg Prifysgol Cymru.

Prosser, H. (1995) Datblygiadau newydd ym maes Cymraeg i oedolion. *Barn* 389, June, 50–51.

Prosser, H. (1996) Cronfa ddatblygu Cymraeg i oedolion. *Y Tiwtor* Summer, 1.

Prosser, H. (1996/7) The teaching of Welsh to adults. *Language Issues* 8(2), 6–7.

Prosser, H. (1997) Teaching Welsh as a second language to adults. In M. Griffiths (ed.) *The Welsh Language in Education* (pp. 95–98). Cardiff: WJEC.

Prosser, H. (2001) Ymweld â Phatagonia. *Y Tiwtor,* Summer, 6.

Prosser, H. (2002) Interview with Lynda Pritchard Newcombe.

Prosser, H. (2003) Interview with Lynda Pritchard Newcombe.

Prosser, H. (2004) Learners' life could be a ball. *Agenda,* Autumn, 81–82.

Prosser, H. (2005) *Yr Wythnos,* 16 January (*S4C*).

Prys Jones, S. (1992) Coming home. In O. Davies and F. Bowie (eds) *Discovering Welshness* (pp. 5–11). Llandysul: Gomer.

Pugh, R. (2005) The language of heaven in the land of legend. *Cambria* 7(3), 40–43.

Rees, C. (1995) Interview with Lynda Pritchard Newcombe.

Rees, C. (2000) Datblygiad yr WLPAN. In C. Jones (ed.) *Cyflwyno'r Gymraeg* (pp. 27–44). Llandysul: Gomer.

Rees, J. (2004) Welsh demands a place at the top table of learning. *Western Mail,* 4 November, 32.

Rhys, E. (1987) *Nantgwrtheyrn.* Llanrwst: Gwasg Carreg Gwalch.

Rhys, E. (1995) Interview with Lynda Pritchard Newcombe.

Rhys, M. (ed.) (1989) *Ar Fy Myw.* Dinas Powys: Honno.

Richards, J.C. and Renandya, W.A. (2002) (eds) *Methodology in Language Teaching.* Cambridge: Cambridge University Press.

Richardson, G. (1983) *Teaching Modern Languages.* London: Croom Helm.

Roberts, F. (2002) Interview with Lynda Pritchard Newcombe.

Roberts, F. and Davies, B. (2002) *Cymathu Dysgwyr yn y Gymuned Gymraeg ei Hiaith.* Papur Cynhadledd Cymdeithas Broffesiynol i Diwtoriaid Cymraeg i Oedolion, 14 Mehefin.

Roberts, G. (1994) Interview with Lynda Pritchard Newcombe.

Roberts, G.W. (1994) Nurse/patient communication within a bilingual health care setting. *British Journal of Nursing* 3(2), 60–67.

Roberts, R. (2002) I Fod yn Frank. *Tu Chwith* 17, 106–110.

Robinson, P. (2002) *Individual Difference and Instructed Language Learning.* Amsterdam: John Benjamins.

Robinson, W.P. and Giles, H. (eds) (2001) *The New Handbook of Language and Social Psychology.* Chichester: Wiley & Sons.

Rodriguez, R. (1981) *Hunger of Memory.* Boston, Massachusetts: David R. Godine.

Rogers, A. (2002) *Teaching Adults* (3rd edn). Buckingham: Open University Press.

Rogers, A. (2003) What's the difference? *Adults Learning* 15(2), 15–17.

Rogers, J. (1992) *Adults Learning.* Milton Keynes: Open University Press.

Rogers, J. (2006) Llook who's talking. *The Guardian* G2, 22 June, 10–11.

Romaine, S. and Nettle, D. (2000) *Vanishing Voices.* Oxford: Oxford University Press.

Rosser, D.K. (1989) The decay of a Welsh-speaking street community: Migration and its residual effects. *Contemporary Wales* 3, 119–135.

Rubin, J. (2002) E-mail communication with Lynda Pritchard Newcombe.

Rubin, J. and Thompson, I. (1982) *How to be a Successful Learner.* Boston: Heinle & Heinle.

Ryder, J. (2004) Interview with Lynda Pritchard Newcombe.

Sadtono, E. (ed.) (1991) *Language Acquisition & the Second/Foreign Language Classroom.* Singapore: Seameo.

Sargant, N. (2000) *The Learning Divide Revisited.* Leicester: NIACE.

Sayer, V. (1998) Learning Welsh. *Books in Wales* 4, 6–8.

Schuchat, T. (1990) *ULPAN: How to Learn Hebrew in a Hurry.* Jerusalem: Gefen.

Schumann, J.H. (1986) Research on the acculturation model for second language acquisition. *Journal of Multilingual and Multicultural Development* 7(5), 379–392.

Scovel, T. (1978) The effect of affect in foreign language learning: A review of the anxiety research. *Language Learning* 28(1), 129–142.

Scovel, T. (2000) *Learning New Languages: A Guide to Second Language Acquisition.* San Francisco: Heinle & Heinle.

Seliger, H. and Long, M. (eds) (1983) *Classroom-oriented Research in Second Language Acquisition.* Rowley, Mass: Newbury House.

Selinker, L. (1972) Interlanguage. *IRAL* 10(3), 209–231.

Selinker, L. (1992) *Rediscovering Interlanguage.* London: Longman.

Shephard, C.A., Howard, G. and Le Poire, B.A. (2001) Communication accommodation theory. In W.P. Robinson and H. Giles (eds) *The New Handbook of Language and Social Psychology.* Somerset, NJ: John Wiley and Sons, pp. 33–56.

Shoaib, A. and Dörnyei, Z. (2001) Affect in lifelong learning: Exploring L2 motivation as a dynamic process. In P. Benson and D. Nunan (2004) *Learners' Stories* (pp. 22–41). Cambridge: Cambridge University Press.

Sidwell, D. (ed.) (1987) *Teaching Languages to Adults.* London: CILT.

Singleton, D. (2001) Age & second language acquisition. *Annual Review of Applied Linguistics* 21, 77–89.

Smith, D. (1984) *Wales! Wales?* London: George Allen & Unwin.

Smith, D. (1987) Modern languages and the adult student. In D. Sidwell (ed.) *Teaching Languages to Adults* (pp. 1–16). London: CILT.

Smoke, T. (1998) (ed.) *Pedagogy & Participation in Classroom and Community Contexts.* Mahwah, New Jersey: Erlbaum.

Stavans, I. (2002) *On Borrowed Words.* Boston: Godine.

Stengal, E. (1939) On learning a new language. *International Journal of Psychoanalysis* 2, 471–479.

Stevick, E.W. (1976) *Memory, Meaning and Method.* Rowley, MA: Newbury House.

Stevick, E.W. (1989) *Success with Foreign Languages.* Hemel Hempstead: Prentice Hall International.

Stevick, E.W. (1996) *Memory, Meaning and Method (2nd edn).* Boston: Heinle & Heinle.

Stonelake, M. and Davies, E. (2006) *Cwrs Sylfaen.* Cardiff: WJEC.

Street, R.L. and Giles, H. (1982) Speech accommodation theory: A social cognitive approach to language and speech behavior. In M. Roloff and C.R. Berger (eds) *Social Cognition and Communication.* Beverly Hills, CA: Sage, pp. 193–226.

Talfryn, I. (2001) *Dulliau Dysgu Ail Iaith.* Dinbych: Popeth Cymraeg.

Tarone, E. (2004) Does social context affect second-language acquisition? The research evidence. Paper given at Iowa State University on 4th March.

Thomas, E.W. (2001) *Gwneud Cymru'n Wlad Ddwyieithog.* Caerdydd: Bwrdd yr Iaith Gymraeg.

Thomas, P. (2001) Learning my own language. *Cambria* 4(3), 18–21.

Thomas, P.W. and Mathias, J. (eds) (2000) *Developing Minority Languages.* Department of Welsh, Cardiff University, with Llandysul: Gomer.

Thomas, R.S. (1997) *Autobiographies.* London: J.M. Dent.

Thomas, S. (2001) *You Don't Speak Welsh!* Talybont Ceredigion: Y Lolfa.

Tremblay, P.F. and Gardner, R.C. (1995) Expanding the motivation concept in language learning. *Modern Language Journal* 79(4), 505–518.
Trosset, C.S. (1984) The social identity of Welsh learners. Unpublished M.A. thesis, University of Austin, Texas.
Trosset, C.S. (1986) The social identity of Welsh learners. *Language in Society* 15(2), 165–191.
Trosset, C.S. (1993) *Welshness Performed.* Tucson: University of Arizona Press.
Trosset, C.S. (2002) E-mail communication with Lynda Pritchard Newcombe.
Tsui, A.B.M. (1996) Reticence and anxiety in 2nd language learning. In K.M. Bailey and D. Nunan (eds) *Voices from the Language Classroom* (pp. 145–167). Cambridge, Massachusetts: Cambridge University Press.
Turner, G. (1976) Ateb dysgwr. *Y Gwyddonydd* 14(2), 50–62.
Unidentified (1982) *Institut für Niederdeutsche Sprache (1972–1982).* Bremen: Institut für Niederdeutsche Sprache.
Unidentified (1998a) Dysgu Cymraeg a dod yn faer. *Y Cymro,* 7 October, 13.
Unidentified (1998b) Sbaeneg gyntaf – Cymraeg wedyn i Wyddeles. *Y Cymro* 26 August, 11.
Unidentified (1999a) Bwyd Bev. *Lingo Newydd* August/September, 12.
Unidentified (1999b) Cymru, Cymry a Caerdydd. *Y Cymro,* 20 January, 15.
Unidentified (2001) Y Nant am ddenu mwy na ddysgwyr Cymraeg. *Y Cymro* 28 July, 5.
Unidentified (2002) London-born woman who fell for the language of love wins learner award. *Western Mail,* 9 August, 8.
Unidentified (2004) Iraqi Kurds aim to learn from Welsh devolution. *Western Mail,* 6 August, 8.
Welsh Assembly Government (2002) *Iaith Pawb.* Cardiff: Welsh Assembly Government.
Wenden, A. (2001) Metacognitive knowledge in SLA: The neglected variable. In M. Breen (ed.) *Learner Contributions to Language Learning: New Directions in Research* (pp. 44–64). Harlow: Pearson Education.
Williams, C. (1997) Colour in the pictures. *Planet* 125, 25–30.
Williams, C.H. (1990) The Anglicization of Wales. In N. Coupland (ed.) *English in Wales* (pp. 19–47). Clevedon: Multilingual Matters.
Williams, C.H. (1994) *Called Unto Liberty.* Multilingual Matters.
Williams, C.H. (ed.) (2000) *Language Revitalisation.* Cardiff: University of Wales Press.
Williams, C.H. (2001) Welsh in Great Britain. In E. Guus and D. Gorter (eds) *The Other Languages of Europe* (pp. 59–81). Clevedon: Multilingual Matters.
Williams, E. (2004) Attracting the Welsh Worm. *Cambria* 6(5), 50–51.
Williams, G. (ed.) (1978) *Social and Cultural Change in Contemporary Wales.* London: Routledge.
Williams, G. and Morris, D. (2000) *Language Planning and Language Use – Welsh in a Global Age.* Cardiff: University of Wales Press.
Williams, I.T. (1965) *Oedolion yn dysgu'r Gymraeg.* Aberystwyth: Cyfadran Addysg, Coleg Prifysgol Cymru.
Williams, I.W. (ed.) (2003) *Our Children's Language.* Talybont, Ceredigion: Y Lolfa.
Williams, J.J. (1994) Attitudes and attained proficiency in Welsh – A study of WLPAN. Unpublished M.A. thesis, University of Wales, Bangor.
Williams, T. (1997) *The Patriot Game.* Beddau: Tynant Books.
WJEC (1992) *Welsh for Adults. The Way Forward.* Cardiff: WJEC.

Woolard, K.A. (1989) *Double Talk: Bilingualism and the Politics of Ethnicity in Catalonia.* Stanford: Stanford University Press.

Worrall, S. (2001) Wales finding its voice. *National Geographic,* June, 62–68.

Worsley, P. (1991) *The New Modern Sociology Readings.* London: Penguin.

Wray, A., Evans, B., Coupland, N. and Bishop, H. (2003) Singing in Welsh, becoming Welsh, 'turfing' and 'grass roots' identity. *Language Awareness* 12(1), 49–72.

Wyn, I. (2001) Cyd-destun Ewropeaidd Amddiffyn y Gymraeg. *Y Faner Newydd* 19, 14–15.

Zar, J.H. (1999) *Biostatistical Analysis* (4th edn). Upper Saddle River, New Jersey: Prentice-Hall International, 449–450.

Index

Authors

Subjects

German 2, 50-51, 60, 96, 109
Get by 47, 56
Globalisation 8, 58
Grammar 15, 27, 30, 67-68, 76, 84, 106
Grammar translation method 27, 40

Hebrew 21, 29, 53

Iaith Gwaith 7
Identity 8, 14, 56-65
Immersion 3, 5, 22, 24
In-migration 65
In-migrant 10, 63-65, 90
Intensive courses19-22, 30-31, 33, 54, 84
Intergenerational transmission 5
Iraqi Kurds 4

Javanese 43, 109

L2 1-2, 14, 23, 28-29, 32, 34, 38, 41-42, 44, 46,
   48, 56, 59-60, 63-64, 66-69, 81-85, 87, 92,
   95, 98, 103, 109, 111-113, 115
Lack of confidence 14, 34, 43, 66-81, 99, 110
Language of wider communication 1, 109,
   116
Language revitalisation 115
Language shift 5, 115-116
Language shock 38, 69
Language switch 39, 42, 46, 49
Lathophobic aphasia 67
Learner diaries xiii, 11, 109
Learner journals xiii, 11, 39, 70, 73, 83, 85,
   89, 101, 113
Learner of the year v, 19, 35, 41, 57, 61, 86,
   90
Learner preparation 14, 84, 105, 112-114
Linguaphone 51, 83
Linguistic diversity 9
Lesser-used languages 2-3, 14, 42, 44, 53, 58,
   80, 85
Luxemburgian 2

Maltese 43
Maori 2-3
Menter Iaith 7
Menter a Busnes 6
Monoglot, 5, 110
Monolingualism 4
Motivation v, xiv, 12, 14, 26, 36, 45-46, 60,
   63, 66, 68, 82, 86-108, 111-113
 – Integrative motivation 12, 87-89, 92-96,
   99-101, 104, 107, 111
 – Instrumental motivation 87-89, 92, 95-96,
   99-104, 107

Multilingual 1, 60
Multilingualism xiii
Mutations 77

Nant Gwrtheyrn 24, 75
Native American languages 2
Native speakers v, xiii, 1, 3, 14, 18-19, 21-22,
   24, 27-28, 33, 39-55, 59, 62-64, 67-68, 74,
   77-81, 86, 92, 98, 103, 105, 109-110,
   112-116
Naturalistic practice 2, 17, 102, 112,
Natural approach 31-32

Patagonia 8, 18-20, 95
Payment by results 4
Plattdeutsch 2
Practice 1-2, 12, 14, 19, 24, 33, 40, 42, 45, 47,
   76, 82, 84 91-92, 104-105, 107, 109 115
Practise v, 15, 18, 21, 31, 34, 39, 41, 43, 48-49,
   52, 54, 66-68, 70-72, 77, 80, 84-86, 98, 111
Practising 14, 42, 48, 54, 80, 82, 86, 99,
   108-109
Protests 5

Radio Cymru 6, 90
Radio Wales 6
Risk-taking 17, 27, 68-70, 77, 107, 114

S4C 6, 25
Silent way 31
SLA xi, 38, 79
Social context 7, 14, 38, 88
Social networks, 1, 37-38
Speed of speech 14, 39, 51-53, 55, 64, 73-74,
   91, 110
Strategies
 – Affective strategies 113
 – Cognitive strategies 113
 – Conversational strategies 113
 – Metacognitive strategies 113
 – Social strategies 113
 – Learner strategies 14, 112-113
Suggestopedia 31-32

Target language 1, 27-28, 30-32, 35, 38, 59,
   64, 67, 74, 87
Ti a Fi 41-42, 49
Total Physical Response 31
Treachery of the Blue Books 4
Twf 7

ULPAN 16, 20-21, 29
ULPANIM 21
Urdd Gobaith Cymru 5, 35